To a true TS

Small Town Baseball

BIG LEAGUE DREAMS

The Best !
Bob Meyer

Bob Meyer

Printed in United States by Lew Printing
Independence, Missouri

Published by Meyer Books

Cover Illustration: Colleen McKeone

Other Credits Not Specifically Notated:

      Baseball Quotes and Trivia: Baseball Almanac and Wikipedia
      Baseball
      Field of Dreams Quotes: Universal Studios
      Pictures and Newspaper Articles: "Dubuque Telegraph-Herald",
      "Dyersville Commercial", "The Golden View"

ISBN #: 978-0515-65475-1

Eighth Printing

DEDICATION

To all past, present, and future players and fans for keeping alive the rich tradition of small town baseball.

CONTENTS

Seventh Inning *S t r e t c h*

INTRODUCTION

My name is Bob Meyer. I was blessed to grow up on a farm in eastern Iowa, near a small community called Balltown, about 20 miles north of Dubuque. Yes, Balltown is its real name. Like most farming communities, people have a good work ethic and a respect for core values. That background has served me well over the years, especially when talent and knowledge were sometimes lacking.

The obvious question: Why write a book on small-town baseball?

For whatever reason, I became interested in the game at an early age, probably five or six. In those post recession and World War II days, there was not much entertainment available to farm kids. Farm work consumed most of our time. There was no Sports Center or televised baseball games because there was no television. Radio was our only media source, so we had to use a lot of imagination while listening to big league games, some of them on ticker tape.

We played pick-up games whenever and wherever we could, which was really limited to grade school fields and farm pastures, anywhere which was semi-level. When not doing farm work, I would hit little rocks with a sawed off broom stick for hours at a time, pretending I was in Wrigley Field or Yankee Stadium. When my brother Roger was old enough we would pitch sponge balls to each other against the machine shed. If we made a little gouge in the ball, we could throw all different kinds of breaking pitches, depending on how we gripped and released the ball. I also read everything on baseball I could, especially "how-to" books and articles on all phases of the game. Collecting baseball cards was another favorite hobby. Since I never attended high school—my own fault—my opportunity to learn the game and develop basic skills did not follow a normal progression. But my passion for the game never wavered, only intensified.

It was that passion that subsequently gave me the privilege of playing highly competitive ball at the military service, college, and semi-pro levels for a combined 17 years. Somewhere early in that time frame, I faced the harsh reality that I would never reach the "BIGS". This realization occurred due to a bad combination: an arm injury while playing baseball in the U.S. Air Force while stationed in San Antonio, Texas and the fact I was simply not good enough. Nevertheless, my love and dedication to the game remained strong. Those years, in a variety of settings, were some of the richest in my life. The thrill of putting on the uniform, lacing up the spikes, and walking onto the ball field was always a privilege. The memory of competing with and against some great ballplayers, as well as class guys, remains with me to this day.

Over the years, I have discovered that I am not unique in retaining those childhood and adult memories. Many other folks also have good memories of being a part of semi-pro baseball in small communities, be they players, fans, umpires, parents, or whatever. That is what this book is about - to recapture those moments and, most importantly, sharing them. The best way to do this is letting other people tell their own stories in their own way. Hopefully, it will help them re-live those special memories and, in the process, share those with everyone interested in amateur and semi-pro baseball.

Just as important, I would hope that present day and future players and fans will appreciate the wholesomeness and innocence of baseball at this non-commercialized level; the beauty of playing purely for love of the game, respecting it, and playing it right!

PREFACE

The purpose of this book is stated in the Introduction. How it came into being requires further explanation. In a word, it was Rich Wolfe.

A native of Lost Nation, Iowa, Rich has published over 45 sports books and is considered the leading sports author in the country. He and I played semi-pro ball one summer for Balltown in the eastern Iowa tournaments, but we had lost touch for a long time. I contacted him after reading several of his books and suggested that Small Town Baseball would be a good book topic. He agreed but suggested that I write it. He even helped with the title—Small Town Baseball...BIG LEAGUE DREAMS. So, although it was my idea, it was Rich who put the wheels in motion and provided guidance along the way.

The more I thought about it and after talking to several former players in the Dubuqueland area, I decided that the interest was definitely there. Many former players and fans still like to reminisce about those good memories. It just seemed the time was right to re-live those memories in writing and to share them with everyone who has ever been interested in small town baseball.

Special recognition has to go to five individuals who have been invaluable in contributing to the project completion: Jerry Roling, Jim Brimeyer, Gene "Tiny" Potts, Joe Sigwarth and Roger Meyer. In addition to giving their wholehearted endorsement, they were instrumental in helping plan the logistics and methodology for obtaining the book's content. So this book is really a collaborative effort involving those individuals and many others throughout this effort.

One of the early decisions was the scope of the book. It was our judgment that we should focus on eastern Iowa since semi-pro ball continues to flourish in that area despite a decline in many parts of the county. So we concentrated primarily on four counties: Dubuque, Delaware, Clayton and Jones. However we reached out to other nearby areas as well. Many players alternated among these other areas as they played on various tournament teams over the years. These include Iowa and Clinton counties as well as the tri-state area states of Illinois and Wisconsin.

Another decision was to ensure a broad representation of towns and people who make up the content. We did not want any one town to be overrepresented insofar as possible. In addition to reaching out to individuals from the various communities, several ads were placed in four local papers inviting anyone who wanted to participate. As a result, everyone who responded and followed through with submitting information is included in some way.

The biggest challenge was deciding what to include in the book. Everyone expressing an interest was interviewed and invited to provide whatever information they desired, including articles and pictures. Naturally, some individuals provided a vast amount of information, stories and pictures. Balancing all the information with the available space resulted in some material that simply could not be included. Likewise, we need to clarify that this book is not a history of semi-pro ball in the eastern Iowa and surrounding counties, nor does it cover the full scope of all people who could also provide interesting stories. It is really a collection of memories and stories of individuals who loved the game and were willing to share those rich experiences.

In the context of memories, a disclaimer is in order. Understandably, everyone has difficulty sometimes in remembering the precise details of incidents and the exact year they occurred. Whenever there was a question on details, including the spelling of a name, an effort was made to obtain the correct fact. However, that was not always possible, so the reader's indulgence is requested if any discrepancy is noted. Likewise, some of the photos are not of the best quality. Every effort was made to obtain the originals, but that was not always possible.

Finally, a heads up to you English teachers and others who are staunch advocates of the proper use of the English language. That stance is very necessary in most literary circles. However, this book tries to capture the memories and stories of people using their own words. And most people, including myself, do not talk like we would write something if that product was meant for a more formal purpose. Therefore, don't expect correct verb conjugation or be surprised if sentences end in prepositions or begin with adverbs. Spontaneity and straight talk was the first priority.

Hope you enjoy it.

Bob

MAP OF EASTERN IOWA

Most of the towns mentioned in this book cover the general area of eastern Iowa,

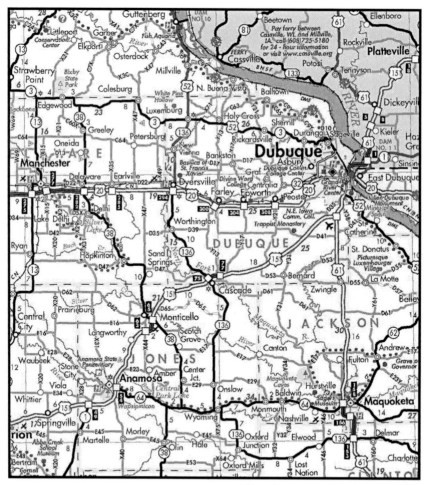

Map reproduced with permission of the Iowa Department of Transportation

"You know what we get to today, Brooks?

We get to play

Baseball."

Dennis Quaid in *The Rookie*, 1981

LASTING MEMORIES

Gary Dolphin is a native of Cascade, Iowa. He is in his 40th year of play-by-play broadcasting, the last 15 years for the University of Iowa football and basketball teams. In addition to six years as the play-by-play announcer for Northwestern University, Gary served as the Network Television Coordinator for the Chicago Bears for ten years. He resides in Dubuque, Iowa and is a Member of the Dubuque County Baseball Hall of Fame.

*M*y first and lasting memories of Dubuque County semi pro baseball are in the late 1950's. Really, it was my introduction to the game I immediately fell in love with.

As a youngster, my first Cascade Red heroes were pitcher Tom Breitbach and slugging right fielder Bob Hoerner. They passed away last summer within two weeks of each other. Before Mickey Mantle, I thought Hoerner was the greatest slugger, period! Breitbach had all the pitches even though he was approaching the twilight of his career.

As bad as I wanted Cascade to beat Dyersville, the Whitehawks had some incredible talent. Art Huinker was the best lefty I can remember from those days, and for his size, Bobby Goldsmith could hit for power. The multi-talented Tom Jenk was a good hitter and could play several positions. Father Wayne Ressler, Popeye Hosch and my uncle, Kenny Kauder, were bigger than life to a kid growing up in Cascade.

What great memories of the Cascade and Dyersville Tournaments in particular, but Dad took my brothers and me to all of them – Worthington, Holy Cross, Rickardsville, and Bernard.

To present day, it's almost astounding how fast time flies as I emcee the annual Dubuque County Baseball Hall of Fame dinner.

1

Here are all these super stars that I either watched or covered, or both, heading to the hall. It makes me appreciate all the great games I witnessed. I'm also appreciative of the tremendous family support that allowed these farmers and factory workers by day, turn into baseball heroes at night!

We are so baseball blessed in Dubuque County.

Gary Dolphin
"Voice of the Iowa Hawkeyes"

Proud Cascade native and baseball fan.

BASEBALL FAMILY

Bob, Joe, and Jim

Jim Hoerner was the third of three brothers who played base-ball in a talented baseball fami-ly. His brother Bob played four years of professional ball in the Chicago Cubs' organization, and is considered one of the best hitters ever to play semi-pro baseball in the tri-state area. His brother, Joe pitched for 14 years in the major leagues with a 2.99 career ERA. All three are members of the Dubuque County Baseball Hall of Fame.

I started playing semi-pro baseball when I was 15 years old. My older brother Bob was a big influence as I was growing up. It was a privilege to catch my brother Joe for three years before he left to play professional ball. He pitched in the major leagues for over 14 years and had an ERA under 3.00 for his entire career. He was the first relief pitcher to ever be selected to an All-Star squad. That was in 1961 when Gil Hodges selected him. He was warming up and ready to go in when Jim Hickman got the game winning hit.

There were eight children in our family - four boys and four girls. My other brother John did not play baseball. We grew up on a farm and he always said he had to stay home and do the farm work while we played baseball. Joe was only a year older than me and we got interested in baseball because of Bob who was nine years older than me. Joe and I would go to the games with him and be bat boys, shag fly balls and things. So it was just kind of bred into us.

When I was a junior at Senior High School in Dubuque we won the state championship in 1954. Joe and Jack Nora did all the pitching and I was the catcher. Of course in those days they didn't play all the games they do now so you could get by with two pitch-ers. Nora also played a couple of years of pro ball with the Dodgers I believe.

3

I started playing semi-pro ball when I was just 15. Most of my playing time was with Key West in the Prairie League and then I played for Cascade in all the tournaments. I also played for Holy Cross and Worthington a couple of times. I played and managed off and on for 34 years, finally giving it up at age 49. When I first started playing for Key West we played in a cow pasture just outside of town. Before each game we would go around with shovels and pick up the cow pies. There was no fence so you really had to earn your home runs.

Then we moved to a ball diamond behind Table Mound Elementary School where the left field foul line was 220 feet to the fence, center field was 500 feet, and right field was 400 feet away. You could hit a long home run and curl it around the left field foul pole and the ball might land 40 feet foul. These days Key West plays their home games in Peosta, Iowa where they have a real nice field.

After I was out of high school for two years, I signed with the White Sox in 1957. I got released in spring training due to an injury. You think you're pretty good around here but when you get down there with all those guys from the Florida and Arizona Instructional Leagues you realize you ain't that good. I remember getting $275 a month. When Joe signed a year earlier he only got $252 a month. I kidded him about that until the day he died. So I came back and started working for the Dubuque Meat Packing Plant where I worked for 43 1/2 years.

I have some great memories playing and managing all those years. There were a lot of good ballplayers and great guys. Some of the better pitchers I remember were Roger Fenwick, Dave Reittinger, Sal Willenbring and Art Huinker. Fenwick pitched 14 games for us in the tournaments and only lost once. Besides my brother Bob, the good hitters I remember were Chick Wegman, Dale Digman, and Father John Moran. Father Moran could have gone a lot further in professional ball but he was a catcher and didn't want to injure his fingers because he wanted to be a priest. I remember whenever he came up, the young kids would go behind the outfield fence because it seemed like he was always hitting home runs.

4

There are a lot of good memories and it is still fun to talk about them. Two of my biggest thrills involved being named MVP in the Worthington Tournament in 1959 where I hit .532 with two home runs and named the MVP. Then, during my last year of managing, my three sons and I were all in the starting line-up together - Mark, Rick, and Mike.

Of course, there are a lot of good stories too. One time I was catching my brother Bob in a game against Peosta. Bob could throw pretty hard and he was throwing all fastballs that game. Their first baseman, Moose Weydert, was a big lefthanded hitter and he was moving farther back in the batters box each time up. He was so far back I thought he was going to take my head off. So I thought we're going to cross him up with a curve ball and he will swing out of his shoes. I called for a curve ball over the outside and it broke right over the heart of the plate. Moose must have hit that ball 500 feet. As he's rounding second base Bob looks into me with a glare and says, "Jimmy come out here." The umpire says, "I think Bob is really ----." I head toward the mound and when I'm about 15 feet away he says in a loud voice, "Take those two fingers and put them you know where!" (He didn't use those exact words.) I came back behind the plate and told the umpire he was right and that I wouldn't be calling for any more curves the rest of the game. If I remember right Bob hit a homerun in the 9th inning and we won the game, so it turned out all right. But he could have shaken me off. I later told him that Peosta and Key West are pretty close together and he didn't have to talk so loud so everyone could hear him.

I used to think I could call a pretty good game because I was always watching the hitters, how they were standing and moving in the batters box. One day this guy from Key West was pitching and he had all kinds of different pitches. But he was always shaking me off and I was getting tired of it. So in about the 3rd inning I called time and went out to the mound and said, "The bases are loaded, there's nobody out and they have three runs in. Your pitches aren't working, why don't you try one of mine?"

Another time when I was managing, Key West was playing in the championship game of the Cascade Tournament. I couldn't be there because I had to go to Colorado the night before. So the guy I picked to manage the team, Bob Gassman, was coaching third base. In the 7th inning he decided to send up a pinch hitter. The guy who was supposed to hit came charging from the on deck circle toward the coaching box and said, "Do you think Jim would do this?" Gassman said, "Do you want me to ask the umpire to call time and delay the game while I go to the phone in the announcing booth and call Jim in Colorado to ask him. Now sit down and shut up!"

I could talk a long time about all these good memories. It's too bad that the interest is not there like it used to be. I think slow pitch softball was a big reason for the decline of baseball, but that's just the way it is.

> *"Ballplayers only have two things to do. Play and keep their mouths shut."*
>
> Sparky Anderson,
> Former Manager of Cincinnati and Detroit

Jerry is kneeling in the second row far left

HOME TOWN BASEBALL
AND HOME TOWN PRIDE

Jerry Roling played most of his semi-pro ball with the Holy Cross town team which had its best years in the 1970s and 1980s. After graduating from Loras College he coached high school baseball his entire career, now numbering 40 years. His total victories to date number over 956. He is presently the baseball coach at Wahlert High School in Dubuque. He is a member of the Dubuque County Baseball Hall of Fame and the Iowa High School Hall of Fame. Jerry was recently honored as National High School Baseball Coach of the Year by the National High School Athletic Coaches Association. The award is based on overall coaching record, professional honors, and contributions to the sport.

What I have to say really represents the feelings of most of the guys that I played with in Holy Cross for many years.

Our interest in baseball started at a very early age, probably eight or nine years old. In addition to games and organized Little League practices, we played two or three pickup games a day on any of one of five different fields. Each field was unique in size, shape, and special ground rules: three outs in the weeds, left field open only, catch the ball out of the trees and you're out, homerun if ball is into the road, double over the fence in right, homerun in the creek etc.

7

When we played on the town team field behind the school, we would "borrow" the team's equipment out of the shed in the apple orchard. The manager, Bob Lake, never knew we used it, or maybe he did. We knew every bat used by the players on his team, including John Schiesel's big 36 inch bat. We imagined ourselves being the big team players on this field. There were two fields on parish grounds and our parish pastor, Rev. John Hemesath, loved baseball and he was very accommodating in letting us use the fields. On the one field, the cemetery was part of fair territory with "Hayes" tombstone as third base. There were some interesting bounces off the tombstones.

On Sunday afternoons when the team played at home, some of us would get there early so we didn't have to pay and we could shag balls in the outfield during batting practice. This was a big deal! Once the game started, we became fans and ball chasers. Each foul ball returned was worth a dime. Many foul balls bounced off the school onto a gravel road. If you could collect a dollar and leave without scraped knees, it was a great day. I always remember Ron LeGrand as being the most aggressive one. We liked it when he wasn't at some of the games so others would have a better chance.

Our Little League season consisted of 15-20 games a summer. The Holy Cross Little League tournament was the highlight of our season. Carl Brimeyer was our coach and also the postmaster of the town. Some of us would hang around there during the day. We had rubber ball games to the side of the post office, with a strike zone painted on the wall. I remember Hank Lucas trying to throw a rubber ball through a cement wall into the strike zone, by the side of his store. He did that religiously, which paid dividend for him throughout his career. Hank later signed a professional contract with the Los Angeles Dodgers under the coaching of Tommy Lasorda. These were formative years in the development of our baseball skills.

After Little League we started playing Babe Ruth ball. Louie Ruden took over as coach and continued to improve our development. The number of games we played increased as well. The highlight of these summers was the Farley Babe Ruth tournament. What a neat memory pulling into the ballpark at Farley for the first time and seeing the grandstand over the bleachers. In that last tournament we beat Dyersville, coached by Art Huinker. The game ended on a controversial play at the plate involving our catcher "Nuts" Roling blocking the plate and making the tag for the final out.

We then went on to Junior Legion ball, also coached by Louie Ruden. Some of us started playing on the town team during that time. Those years also coincided with the high school seasons. In my freshmen year, Dubuque Wahlert was ranked #1 in the state and came to Holy Cross for a game on their schedule. For some reason, the game was not on our schedule so when they showed up we were practicing in blue jeans. We were willing to play the game if they were okay with us not being in uniform. The decision was made to play and rumor has it that our coach went over to the tavern to get two umpires. We beat Wahlert 7-6 with my brother Ralph and Bill Sigwarth doing the pitching. But Wahlert got revenge in the state tournament beating us 5-1 behind Bill Burbach, who went on to pitch for the Yankees.

In my senior year of high school, Norway beat us in the semi finals 4-2 in ten innings. Hank Lucas and Dan "Hooks" Schmitt pitched us through the tournament to that game. Hooks and Dick McVay hooked up in a 1-1 deadlock through nine innings. They scored three unearned runs in the top of the tenth and we had one run in the bottom of the inning. Hank Lucas narrowly missed a walk-off three run homer that just went foul.

After high school I played four years at Loras College which has had some very good baseball teams over the years. In my senior year we missed going to nationals by one game. Many eastern Iowans have contributed to their success. In that last year, six of the eight position starters and three of the top pitchers were from eastern Iowa. Those days, as well as now, baseball has been a hotbed in eastern Iowa and across the river.

The semi-pro scene has left many great memories over the years. The most rewarding part of this experience has been the friendships formed with teammates as well as opponents in reliving the memories of great games. Bob Roling was our coach for all those years

9

and did a great job. He would twist his hat when he wasn't satisfied with what he was seeing on the field. Our most successful teams were the ones in the 70s and early 80s. We felt our team had some talent with great chemistry and a lot of hometown pride. The final score was much more important than individual stats. We didn't even keep stats back then. Most of our players were hometown, with a few coming from nearby Luxemberg. Baseball was a way of life for us in those days.

The Dyersville tournament was always the highlight of the summer tournament trail. Sometimes there were over 5,000 people during the queens' night and finals. Many teams hired players for tournament games, especially this one. Even as a spectator, starting when I was a Little League batboy, I enjoyed watching all those great players. During our good years, we faced many hired pitchers. We enjoyed the challenge of facing the best pitchers, whether they were fresh of the college scene or a crafty veteran. The better the competition, the better we liked it. But we always stuck with our own team, including pitching. This contributed to a large fan base which, in turn, contributed to our success.

Some Neat Stories

We made trips to Monticello for tournaments and the Jones County Fair baseball game. Monti had the most renowned bat boy in the area, John Ferring. Back when All-Star wrestling was popular, John and Hank Lucas would always claim to have the belt. We would show up at the park and John would always say he had the belt and Hank would say: "You have the mouth and I have the belt." One day after a game and a few drinks, a tag team match was set up between John and Dan Reid vs. Hank and Tim Hayes. Of course, we were all good friends and this was all done in fun. Anyway, during the match, Hank threw a punch, intentionally trying to miss, but John moved right into it. He was temporarily stunned and went down for the count. The match ended there, but the debate continued as to who had the belt.

We were playing at Balltown one Sunday afternoon. Bill Pins hit a home run late in the game that could have won it for us. But the umpire ruled it foul, sighting a birdhouse pole as the foul pole

10

rather than the actual foul pole. That game is still known as the "birdhouse" game.

One hot sunny afternoon at Holy Cross, Dorrance Melloy was umping behind the plate. He turned to our bench and asked for some new baseballs. Hank took an old ball and put it in the white chalk bag to make it look new. A couple of pitches later Dorence asked for a new ball. He took his mask off before catching it. He caught it and "Puff", white chalk all over his sweaty face.

We showed up at Otter Creek one day and home plate was in backward. In another park the pitching rubber was 66' from home plate instead of 60' 6". This was discovered as I was warming up and realized my curve ball never got to the plate.

I've had some tremendous experiences playing and coaching this great game of baseball! I feel very fortunate to have played with some of the best teammates in the world and playing against some great ballplayers during all those years. Of all those players, I would say Art Huinker was the best all-around player. He could do it all.

> *"All right everybody, line up alphabetically according to your height."*
>
> Casey Stengel

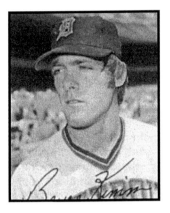

FROM SMALL TOWN BASEBALL
TO THE MAJOR LEAGUES

Bruce Kimm is a native of Norway, Iowa where he starred in high school baseball and basketball. He played and coached a combined 34 years in professional baseball, 17 in the major leagues. He was interim manager with the Chicago Cubs for part of the 2002 season, and retired from professional baseball after the 2003 season as third base coach with the Chicago White Sox. He and his wife Deborah make their home in Amana, Iowa.

I became interested in baseball at a very early age. My dad and cousin Wayne always played catch with me. While in grade school I played Little League and Pony League ball until high school As soon as I was old enough I was batboy for the Norway town team. I would also be the bat boy for visiting teams like Slater when they came in to play Norway or Watkins.

Growing up, my idol was Allan Schulte. He was seven years older than me and I just looked up to him because of the way he trained. He had such a great work ethic. He put all his efforts into sports, especially baseball. He tried to give himself the chance to be the best he could be. He was the star player at the high school when I was in Little League. I would always see him run to and from practice because he ran right past my house on the way to the high school. Most of the guys would walk or drive, but Al always ran. He never drank or smoked or anything like that. I looked up to him as an example and that always stayed with me

It wasn't until I was 14 that I started catching. Before that I played every position. The town team catcher got hurt or something, so they needed a catcher. They talked it over and thought I was too small, but they decided to give it a try. At first, I wasn't interested in catching but it was a chance for me to play so I did it. The first game was against Newhall and I had a good game. I think I went two for three and caught Butch Boddicker who was throwing a knuckleball. So that is how I became a catcher and learned to love it because I was in on every pitch. In high school, I played on the high school team, the junior legion team and the town team, all at the same time. We won two state high school baseball championships when there was only one division and we had only 121 students in the whole school. We also won four state fall championships.

Playing town baseball with Norway was really great. We had good talent in Norway and always could field a team with locals, except we occasionally would bring in a pitcher to pitch in the Watkins or Norway tournaments. The Iowa Valley League was very competitive with teams like Watkins, Williamsburg, Keystone, Fairfax and some others. Watkins always had good teams and then they would pick up other players to make them even better.

One of my biggest thrills was playing for Balltown in the Dyersville tournament before my senior year in high school. I remember I played two games, and I will never forget the long home run to deep left center off Art Huinker who was pitching for Dyersville. I can still see the pitch, a thigh high fastball on the inner half of the plate. He had a reputation for being such a great pitcher so it was quite a thrill for a young guy like me. I also remember the huge crowd. People were sitting on the grass down both foul lines. There were great crowds when Norway and Watkins played, but nothing like that. I think we lost to Dyersville 10-9.

Scouts started noticing me during my sophomore year in high school because they were following Dick McVay who was a year older than me. He was the greatest athlete to ever come out of Norway. Of course, I never saw Hal Trosky play, and Mike Boddicker was great in his own right. But McVay was just fantastic. He was only 5' 10" but he could dunk a basketball. The scouts were following him pretty close and they started to notice me. Even though I wasn't very big, I was known as a scrapper and I could hit, catch, and play the game.

So I signed with the White Sox right out of high school. That was the beginning of a very rewarding 34 year career in professional baseball. I can best describe it as, "It was quite a ride." One thing I still take pride in is that I was known in professional circles as "Gamer". I loved to give all I had to try to win the game. Breaking up double plays was something I always took pride in.

Even with all the wonderful memories of professional ball, I still remember those good memories of semi-pro ball. For a number of years, before I was in the majors, I would come home and looked forward to playing for Norway in the tournaments at Norway and Watkins after the minor league season was over. Of course, I had to adjust to the pitching because it was not as good as what I was used to in professional ball, but it was fun.

Some of the good players that I remember from those semi-pro years were guys like Rocky Rothrock from Watkins, Al Albers from Keystone, Joe Zahn an outsider who pitched on occasion for Norway, Duke Lee from Norway and played for Iowa, and of course, Butch Boddicker. Rothrock was the best. He knew how to pitch and I can recall guys saying that he could turn it up a notch when he got in trouble. He was also a very nice man.

I had a great career in baseball and semi-pro ball was a big part of it.

Editor's Note: For a detailed bio on Kimm search the internet for a lengthy article that Bill Johnson wrote for a SABR (Society for American Baseball Research) newsletter after Bruce retired from baseball. Search www.sabr.org

A BASEBALL FAMILY TREE

Lee Simon was born and raised on a farm in the Fillmore, Iowa area. He still lives in that area and works for the John Deere Dubuque Tractor Works. He is a member of the Dubuque County Baseball Hall of Fame.

*B*aseball was always a big thing with my family. I come from a big family of eleven children, five brothers and five sisters. Can you imagine raising eleven children today? How would you get them in a car, with all the car seats and everything? Of course, in those days there weren't many other things to do so we always played baseball. My dad played baseball and my grandfather played baseball. Matter of fact, my grandfather had eight older brothers and they all played baseball. From 1905 to 1907 they all played together around the Bankston area. They were called the Simon Nine. My grandfather was the pitcher. My dad and his brothers played together, and my brothers and I all played together. I went to a one room school until the sixth grade and we played baseball until the snow flew.

Then I went to St. Martins for a few years and then went to Aquin High School. I was one of the lucky ones. I had a different baseball coach every year, but the best one was Bob White. He was a good pitcher and a pretty good ballplayer. In fact, he pitched for different teams in the tournaments around here.

I played my first town team game when I was 15. That was in 1957. Placid had just won the semi final game in the Worthington Tournament. But they were short of players for the championship game because a number of the guys had reserve duty. Dan Irvin was the manager and he said to me the night before, "Get ready, you're playing tomorrow night." He was my uncle. That's all he said, "You're playing tomorrow night." Of course, I wasn't real concerned because I'd been watching them play ever since I was seven or eight years old. I played second base and we won 5-3. We had five hits and I had one of them.

Then one day, Cascade played at the Monticello Fair and they were short of players. So I played left field and a funny thing happened that day. Popeye Hosch was playing shortstop. Anyway, a short fly ball was hit out toward left field and both Popeye and I were going after it and started calling for it right away. Of course, I'm only 15 but I know how this game is supposed to be played - the outfielder has the easier play so he should take it. So I called for it, then Popeye calls for it, then I call for it and Popeye calls for it and I call again, "I got it, I got it." Finally he backs away and said, "Okay, but don't drop it kid." That really tests your confidence, but I caught it. If you know Popeye he was a pretty rough and gruff guy. In fact, he always had the reputation for not touching first base on extra base hits. He would cut that base short and head for second, at least against certain teams when he knew he could get away with it. Of course, the players and umpires were watching the ball in the outfield and didn't see him do it. But he was a good hitter and a good ballplayer.

One of the funniest stories I remember was a game in the Worthington tournament in the late 1950s or early 1960s. Bernard was playing Epworth who had a bunch of older guys playing like Jerry Dougherty, Ralph McDermot, Ralph Buchman and those guys. Bernard brought in two guys from Notre Dame, a pitcher and a first baseman named Bob Bentley. The pitcher gets knocked out early and they brought Bentley in to pitch. He must have been a fourth or fifth string pitcher or something. Man could he throw hard, but he didn't know where the ball was going. In those days very few of those Epworth guys wore helmets. But after seeing some of Bentley's warm up pitches go half way up the screen and then seeing some of his pitches go behind batters' heads, everybody was scrambling for helmets and being pretty edgy at the plate. Ralph McDermott was batting and Buchman was coaching third. He could see that Ralph was a little uneasy up there, so he hollers in: "Get in there and dig in." Ralph steps out of the batters box and yells back, "All right you red headed bastard, here's the bat."

There were a lot of good ball players that I remember over the years. I remember one night when I was still pretty young, mom and dad and some of us kids were out somewhere. On the way home we were coming through Worthington and the ball park lights were on, so we pulled in. They could park cars on the road beyond the right field fence so we parked there and started to watch the game. Well, the announcer said that the next batter would be Jack Dittmer and my dad said we might see a ball come out here because he had played for the Milwaukee Braves. Sure enough, about the second or third pitch he hits a home run and it went into the ditch along where we're parked. Kids came out looking for it and they couldn't find it so we go over and pick it up because we saw where it landed. Having a good ball was a great thing so we probably used it the rest of the year until it was worn out.

Another good ballplayer I remember when I was young was Haven Schmidt. He had played Double A or Triple A ball in the Cincinnati organization for a number of years but got tired of living out of a suitcase and decided he was going to come back to Iowa to farm and milk cows. Winky Hoerner was the manager of Zwingle and talked him into playing for them for a few years in the tournaments. I remember one tournament at Cascade he hit three home runs. He is the only player that I know of who won the MVP Award for a third place team. I also remember a night in the Dyersville Tournament in the early sixties when his team was playing Independence. Independence always had hired pitchers and I think their pitcher that night was Doug Rider, I'm not sure. But he was a good pitcher. Anyway Independence is ahead by a few runs and the bases were loaded for the other team. Haven was due up and the Independence manager goes to the mound and is talking to the pitcher and catcher and a couple of the infielders. The pitcher keeps shaking his head "no" and you knew what they were talking about. That pitcher was saying, "I ain't gonna walk him, I ain't gonna walk anybody." They could afford to walk Haven and still have a decent lead. But this pitcher refused to give in so the manager goes back to the dugout. On either the first or second pitch Haven hits a shot that hit the scoreboard that was over the right centerfield fence. The scoreboard had a lot of tin in it and when that ball hit it, you could hear the echo all over the ballpark. It was a grand slammer which put them in the lead and Independence lost the game.

Jim McAndrew from Lost Nation was some kind of pitcher. I saw him strike out 23 hitters in a tournament game against Pleasant Grove at Lowden. Pleasant Grove had good teams those years and he struck out all those guys.

Art Huinker, there was another good one. I saw him one time after he quit playing and asked when he decided to hang them up. He said, "Remember Bruce Kimm? He was just a kid then. When he hit that ball over the 425 sign by the flag pole, I knew now is the time to get out." Kimm used to come back and play for Norway after his minor league season was over. My brother was playing third base for somebody down there and Bruce went five for five. He hit some shots by my brother and my brother says to the pitcher, "Jesus, keep that ball away from him".

Besides McAndrew and Huinker, some other good pitchers were Ed Sawville, Dick McVay, and Dave Reittinger. I caught Sawville in the Dyersville Tournament against Winthrop, and man could he throw. After warming him up before the game I went to the dugout and looked at their lineup. I saw that Carl Blumenshine was batting seventh. I thought to myself, what is this, a guy like that batting that far down in the lineup? But I want to tell you, they never touched him. He was from south of here, down around Wyoming or some place like that. I batted against Dick McVay and he was tough. He played at Norway about the same time as Bruce Kimm was there, but he signed right out of high school so I never got to see him after that. Reittinger from Dyersville was one of the best. When his curve ball was on he could just buckle you.

It's hard to name the best ball player I ever saw around here, but I would have to say Art Huinker because he was so good all around. As far as hitters, there have been a lot of good ones. Some that come to mind are Bob Hines and Gordy Westhoff from Monticello, Dick Wold, and Haven Schmidt. Of course, Dyersville always had a good outfit and they were all good hitters. Tom Jenk was a good hitter, but I never saw him in his prime. Mick Meyer and Larry Conrad were also very good; they had beautiful swings.

I guess I was a pretty good hitter who could hit the long ball once in a while. Down at Bernard one day, I hit one over the 429 sign in centerfield and the centerfielder from Farley, one of the Steffen boys, reached over and caught it. I couldn't believe it. He made one heckuva play. No one had ever hit one out of there. I hit it right down central and I thought that baby was gone. But you got to realize that was with an aluminum bat. God, I hated those bats! That was the worst thing they ever did when they started using that crap. They were a joke. Guys who were singles and doubles hitters suddenly started hitting home runs. Get this. The first year they returned to wood bats in the Cascade Tournament in the early 90s, there was only one home run during the whole tournament. The year before that, there were 36. What does that tell you?

Probably my biggest thrill was in the Cascade Tournament when I was just 16 years old. I had the most hits, the highest batting average and was named the MVP. The next youngest guy to win the MVP at Cascade was Kevin Rhomberg from Dubuque when he was only 17. Anyway, one of the Westhoff boys from Monticello told me, "Don't accept any money, whatever you do, because you will no longer be an amateur." Even though it was only $10 he said my dad should go someplace else and accept it, but I could not do it.

The Simon Brothers - 1981
Merlin (deceased), Loras, Matt, Lee, Irwin, Tom

In 1972, Rod Carew was the American League batting champion, but he did not hit a single home run.

HAVE GLOVE AND BAT—
WILL TRAVEL

Dick Wold is a native of Monono, Iowa. He attended Upper Iowa University. Taught and coached in high school for 35 years. Dick resides with his wife Beth in Maquoketa, Iowa.

I got interested in baseball when I could barely walk, knee high to a grasshopper you might say. My dad and two brothers played all the time. One would pitch and another would hit and we just kept doing that.

Played little league in the Monona area. A guy by the name of Gary Peterson was our coach. He really kept baseball going there for a long time. It seemed like we had at least one game every day. Then as a sophomore in high school I began playing semi-pro ball with the Monona town team. We played teams like Osage, New Hampton, St. Lucas, Allison, and Festina with the Huinker boys. They had some good ball up there but nothing like down around Dyersville and Watkins and Williamsburg.

When I was a senior in high school I played for Guttenberg in the Dyersville tournament. That would have been in 1962. Guttenberg had great ball clubs those years, with guys like Al Klinger, Duane Hagan, Merle Hyde, Rod Tangeman and Bruce Hinkle. Herb Borcherding was our manager.

After high school I went to college at Upper Iowa and played three years before being drafted by the Twins. I went to spring training in their rookie league in Minnesota that first year and then went to their regular spring training in Texas the next year. I was released after spring training. I didn't have enough power. I started out playing first base and their number two draft choice was a guy by the name of Jerry Graham. They gave him a bunch of money and moved me to the outfield, and I didn't have a prayer.

I eventually ended up in Maquoketa where I taught and coached in high school for 33 years. Maquoketa had a team in the Prairie League at that time so I played for them. I also played a couple of years for Anchor Bay in Wisconsin, in a good semi-pro league around Madison I also played at various times in different tournaments with teams like Epworth, Hopkinton, Monticello, Rickardsville, Bernard, Key West and Guttenberg. That was when those tournaments really drew a lot of fans. I remember walking out of Dyersville one queens night with Rocky Rothrock who had just pitched a shutout, and it seemed like we were walking over and kicking beer cans all the way out. It was just unreal.

Playing semi-pro ball was so much more fun than playing professional ball. My biggest thrills were playing for Williamsburg in the NBC Tournament and different times for Watkins and Dyersville in the ABC Tournament. Doc Miller from Williamsburg got every player he could from different parts of the country, but we could never beat Clarinda and Slater so we never went to the national tournament in Wichita. When playing for Dyersville in the ABC tournament in Battle Creek, Michigan I roomed with Jim McAndrew who later had a successful career with the New York Mets.

Some of the best pitchers I faced over the years were Dennis Leonard, Eddie Watt, Rich Folkers and Vern Geishert. Leonard, Folkers and Watt had successful major league careers. Geishert was out of the University of Wisconsin and pitched one year with the California Angels. Rocky Rothrock who pitched for Watkins and other teams around Dyersville was also very good. He just knew how to pitch. Two of the better hitters I remember were Merle Hyde and Al Klinger who played for Guttenberg. As far as the best all around player, I would have to say Art Huinker. He could do it all.

One of the funniest stories I can remember occurred down at Miles, Iowa one hot Sunday afternoon. It was over 90 degrees. I will never forget it. I was playing for Zwingle and Al Denlinger was our manager. Al never played very much in those days but one day he had to play because two young guys from Dubuque didn't show up by game time. Evidently they had been out the night before partying. Anyway, Al is playing right field and there was no fence out

24

there. Early in the game a guy hits a ball over Al's head and it hit a cement pad and rolled down a long sidewalk. It just kept rolling and rolling and Al runs after it. The batter could have walked around the bases twice before Al finally got to the ball. When he came in after the inning he was out of breath, and these two guys had just pulled up in their car. Al's face was so red and he was so mad he went to their car and really lit into them. I can't repeat what he said but he used every name in the book. The players never got out of the car but turned around and went back to Dubuque.

"I got players with bad watches-they can't tell midnight from noon."

Casey Stengel

SHERRILL BASEBALL LORE

For two decades, Clete Schmitt was a mainstay infielder for Sherrill Baseball. He and his wife Judy reside in Dubuque, Iowa.

Baseball in Sherrill, Iowa was begun and prompted by the Saint Peter and Paul Catholic parish priest and baseball fanatic, Fr. Leo Entringer. In 1953, he bulldozed and graded the first ball diamond in Sherrill on parish grounds. Unfortunately Father wasn't able to enjoy his favorite sport of baseball for very long; he died of leukemia one year later in 1954.

The umpires that Sherrill hired in the 1950's were paid a meager five dollars per game. That stipend rose to $14 per game by the 1970's. The team was able to cover the cost of umpires and equipment by "passing the hat," which brought in $30 to $40 per game. During the "big" games against town teams from Rickardsville and Balltown, the crowd sometimes grew to 50-75 fans. In the fall of 1971, lights were installed to allow the team to play night games. The town team's last year of competing was in 1995. Since then, the field has been used for little league, Babe Ruth, and boys and girls softball competition.

A few specific incidents are cemented in Sherrill Baseball lore. Foul balls, hit over the back-stop required fans to chase them and return them to the bench for reuse. Sometimes the fans who returned the balls were even rewarded a nickel per ball. During one night game, however, one of the loyal Sherrill fans drank a little too much "home brew" and he shagged all the foul balls himself. For some unknown reason, he hid the balls in his car. When the seventh inning came around, no baseballs could be found, and the game had to be delayed until a team scavenger hunt found the balls in the shagger's car. The discovery of the missing balls finally allowed the game to go on.

Quitting or giving up were never words to be associated with Sherrill baseball. In one game, Sherrill was playing rival Dyersville, and the score was 52-2 in favor of Dyersville. The Dyersville manager asked the Sherrill skipper, Norb Kutsch, if he thought it would be a good idea to stop the game. Kutsch replied, "We don't quit in Sherrill." After another couple of innings, the game finally ended, 52-2.

In a memorable game in the Holy Cross Tournament in 1964, Bill Burbach, who later pitched for the New York Yankees, was pitching for Sherrill. Bill consistently threw in the 90's. By the third inning, Sherrill catcher Jerry Schueller's left palm was so sore from catching Burbach's fireballs that Schueller had to remove himself from the game. Jimmy Oberfoell was asked to take Schueller's catching spot. Unfortunately, Jimmy was ill-prepared for the job. He did not wear a protective cup, and the first warm-up pitch from Burbach caught Jimmy squarely in the groin, which sent him to the ground in a fetal position and moaning for the longest five minutes of his life.

Late in the same game, Burbach walked a batter. With Sherrill's Bob Pfohl holding the runner at first base, Burbach fired a dart at Pfohl in an attempt to pick off the runner. The ball was fired so hard that Pfohl didn't even get leather on it, and the ball sailed over the fence beyond first base. The runner moved to second.

These are just some of the unique stories that surround Sherrill baseball. Those were times of great camaraderie, friendship, fun, love of the great game of baseball, unforgettable memories, and a few "brewskis" after the game, win or lose.

"By the time you know what to do, you're too old to do it."
Ted Williams

POWERFUL LESSON

Jim Brimeyer has a Bachelors Degree and Masters Degree from Loras College in Dubuque, Iowa. He has taught English for 44 years, one year at Beckman High School in Dyersville, Iowa, 25 years at Wahlert High School in Dubuque, and 18 at North Iowa Community College in Peosta, Iowa. Jim and his wife Kay reside In Dubuque.

After playing high school and college baseball together, Jim Noonan and I umpired high school, college, and semi-pro baseball in the Dubuqueland area for 20 years. We were honored to umpire the Iowa High School State Tournament and the Iowa High School All-Star series, plus many semi-pro tournament games.

One of the most memorable and inspiring situations we experienced occurred on June 19, 1981, in Maquoketa, Iowa. Maquokata High School was playing Independence High School for the top spot in their conference. The teams were superbly coached by two baseball gentlemen, Curt Nelson of Maquoketa and Lyle Leinbaugh of Independence. The occurrence in the second inning of game two of the double-header on a June night proved that, despite the negative press so many teenagers receive for poor errors of judgment, some young people are great and can teach the adult population some good lessons.

The outfield fence at Maquoketa's ball park was surrounded by a four-foot high, cyclone fence which made umpires' rulings of home runs versus doubles quite a challenge. In the bottom of the second, Maquoketa had runners on first and second with one out. The Maquoketa batter drove a ball to deep left-center. I was umpiring the bases and was positioned behind the pitcher's mound for the play. Upon contact, I ran to the outfield to try to position myself to get the best view possible of the long drive. From my vantage point, I ruled the play a double, which would allow one Maquoketa runner to score, the other runner to stop at third base, and the batter to stop at second. Curt Nelson, the Maquoketa coach, respectfully questioned the ruling saying from his vantage point in the third base coaching box, the ball had clearly left the field in the air, which should have been ruled a homerun, scoring three runners. Because of the difficult view the cyclone fence presented, I did feel somewhat apprehensive about the call. Therefore, I consulted my partner, Jim Noonan, who was calling balls and strikes, to see if he had a better angle on the flight of the ball. Noonan logically stated, "You were a lot closer to the situation than I was from behind home plate."

To try to be as fair as possible and get an accurate call, I decided to do a rare thing in umpiring circles. I said to the two coaches, "I'm going to do one more thing. After this, the play will stand." I then jogged to center field and asked Independence centerfielder, Chris McCalley, "Did that ball go over the fence in the air, or did it bounce over for a ground rule double?" Without hesitation, McCalley responded, "Sir, in all honesty, the ball went over the fence on the fly." I turned to the infield and gave the homerun circle sign above my head and scored all three runners.

Maquoketa went on to win the game. But McCalley's honesty and integrity won the admiration and respect of every person at that ball field. At times, athletics seems to be a "win at all costs" proposition. So it was refreshing and encouraging to find this young man, his coach, and teammates demonstrate priorities of sportsmanship, honesty, and integrity unequaled in games we umpired. British poet Alexander Pope wrote, "An honest man is the noblest work of God." Centerfielder Chris McCalley proved that on June 19, 1981, a day in our umpiring experience we will always remember.

> *"I've never questioned the integrity of an umpire, only his eyesight."*
> Leo Durocher

AN ILLUSTRIOUS CAREER

Tom Jenk Sr. has lived his entire life in Dyersville, Iowa. After serving in the U.S. Air Force, Tom received his Law Degree from Drake University in Des Moines. He returned to his home town and established his own law firm, where he continues an active practice.

*T*he baseball career of Tom Jenk, Sr. has spanned over 67 years. He started playing at the age of 14 and continued playing actively for 28 years. This included stints at the University of Iowa, Dow Air Force Base (while in military service), Drake University, and Dyersville. It was with the semi-pro Dyersville Whitehawks where Tom spent most of his playing time, retiring at the age of 42. During much of that time he also managed the team.

After retiring as manager in1984, Tom's baseball career was far from over. Four years later, he became an assistant coach for the Dyersville Beckman High School team, coached for many years by his son, Tom, Jr. He remained in that position for 25 years until re-tiring this year. In 2004 the Dyersville Commercial Park was named Jenk Field, in honor of Tom Sr. and Tom Jr. for their many years of contribution to Dyersville baseball. This past year, Tom Sr. was recognized by the Iowa High School Baseball Association for 55 years of leadership and devotion to high school baseball.

Jenk's accomplishments in semi-pro baseball are also notewor-thy. His Whitehawks captured three state amateur titles, 1961-63, and the 1962 team finished runners-up at the national finals in Battle Creek, Michigan. He hit over .400 and was named to the All Ameri-can first team. In 1963, Tom was selected for the United States team which participated in the Pan American Games in Brazil. The U.S. squad won a silver medal and Tom hit .353 during the games. He also served three terms as a member of the United States Olympic Baseball Committee, 1973-76.

It was the playing and leadership abilities of Jenk, Sr. which made the Dyersville Whitehawks a perennial power in the eastern Iowa area over four decades, 1950's-1980's. They set the bar high which made all competing teams better because to beat Dyersville was always a real accomplishment and resulted in great pride for the victors.

Asked to name his greatest thrill, Tom says, "There's so many, but just to play ball was always a thrill." His idols growing up were Tom Breitbach and Bob Hoerner. "Not only were they great ballplayers, but they were class guys and I always enjoyed being around them."

Is this legal?

Tom Jenk, Sr. took the game of baseball seriously. But he also liked to have some fun while playing it. Here he grabs the seat of Balltown base runner Dick Dupont's pants to help "hold" the runner at first.

"I could have played another year, but I would have been playing for the money and baseball deserves better than that."
George Brett

BUENIE BASEBALL

Norb "Hooks" Tressel played semi-pro baseball for many years, most notably in North Buena Vista. He later was one of the respected semi-pro umpires in the Dubuqueland area.

*N*orth Buena Vista, "Buenie", is a town of less than a hundred people about 25 miles north of Dubuque. We competed in the Prairie League in the late1950's. I played centerfield during that time and loved roaming the outfield. My teammate in right field and I had to be very careful on balls hit into right and right center fields. First, right field was very short, about 230 feet, and second, the outfield fence was barbed wire. Beyond the fence was a farm field for grazing cattle.

I remember seeing a right fielder chase a ball into the right center gap, only to get his baseball pants caught on the barbed-wire fence and ripped wide open and drawing blood from his leg. Also, when a ball was hit over or through that right field fence, it was difficult to retrieve because we couldn't see the ball in the deep brush and thistle grass, and sometimes the cattle, especially the bull, were not friendly when we tried to retrieve the baseballs.

To get to the Buenie field, we had to drive down a steep dirt road that we entered between Walter Brimeyer's General Store and Joe Bauer's Post Office. The road curved around a hill and past the town dump called the "Blue Hole," which threw out some nasty odors on hot Sunday afternoons late in July and early August. Fans would drive their cars down the hill to the ball field and park along the first base line. At least once or twice a season, a high foul ball went back into this parking area and shattered a windshield and brought forth a bit of foul language from the car's owner.

Spectators would sit on the hoods of their cars or on the dirt road into the ball field to watch the games. Buenie was known for its beer consumption, and the few fans who came to the games usually lived up to that reputation. In fact, it was common to hear the fans harass the umpires on every call they disapproved of. A common barb was, "Hey ump, you better start callin' 'em right. You gotta' get past us to get home!" But no incident ever occurred. In fact, the fans shared their beer with umpires after each game, and they all seemed to have a great time.

After my playing days, I umpired for several seasons in the Prairie League. The games were played on Sunday afternoons. I especially remember two baseball fields, Zwingle and Springbrook that presented some problems for both umpires and players. Zwingle, located about 15 miles south of Dubuque, had a ball diamond located in a cow pasture. The backstop was so poor that foul tips and wild pitches would end up in the creek that flowed behind home plate, which caused some of the balls to become waterlogged and harder for players to throw.

Also, during the course of every game in Zwingle, usually around the seventh inning, we umpires had to call a long time out because a herd of cows would cross the outfield, heading home to be milked. After they slowly made their way across the field, we could resume play. But the outfielders then had to be very careful to avoid the cow pies that were left by the passing herd.

In more recent years, the Zwingle team has had the good fortune to play on a re-designed, up-to-date baseball facility named Loras Collins Field in honor of the man who gave so much of his time, energy, and dedication to baseball in Zwingle. Naming the field after Loras Collins was so well-deserved because he was such a class act and good person who lived for small town baseball in Zwingle.

The Springbrook field was also located south of Dubuque, but in a hay field with no outfield fence. A corn field met the ball field in center field, and if a ball were hit into that corn field, there were no ground rules to stop the hitter at a double, so he could run all day. But that's the way the Springbrook players wanted it. In addition, neither the home plate umpire nor the base umpire could see the right field foul line because that foul line went sharply downhill and turned to the right. We umpires had to guess on fair or foul balls hit down that right field line. One particular Sunday, a batter hit a ball down that right field line. I called it foul, and the Springbrook manager came out and said, "That ball was fair. I could see it from the bench." But I stuck by my call. After the game, I went to the bench and stood on it to see if I made the right call. Even from that position, I could not see the right field foul line. So I said to the manager, "I can't see that foul line. How did you see that it was fair or foul?" He answered, "I didn't really see it. I just wanted to see if I could get you to change the call.

Those are just some of my memorable adventures as a Buenie player and a Prairie League umpire. We didn't get paid much to ump a game, but we sure had a good time with baseball in eastern Iowa.

"We're supposed to be perfect our first day on the job and then show constant improvement."

Ed Vargo, Major League Umpire

CHILDHOOD MEMORY

Joe Sigwarth was born and raised near Balltown, Iowa where he and his brother Leon lived and farmed the family farm. Joe played on the Balltown town team for a number of years and then managed for several years. His son Joey followed his father's footsteps and has managed the team for the last 12 years. Joe has recently published a book titled Vision for the Nearsighted

*T*he scene is small town Balltown, Iowa. An eighth grade elementary school of approximately 70 students, St. Francis has a tradition of playing a baseball game against a neighboring parish, St. Joseph in Rickardsville. Each year the field alternated with home and away. This particular year it was away. Both teams were made up of boys mostly from farms in each community.

I was one of the younger students, a fifth grader. Our teams' strength was hidden in the talent of our 14 year old pitcher, my brother Leon. He had a strong arm who could bring it; he also had good ball movement and excellent control. Now this advantage posed a problem as no one in the upper grades could catch him. Several tried, only to end up with bruises and injuries as the ball frequently caromed off their body. But there was a solution to this dilemma, his younger brother, myself. I could catch him quite handily as I was used to his deliveries while frequently playing catch in our farm yard.

This also posed a problem because permission was needed for a middle school player to play in the game. That permission was denied by my teacher, Sister Rita Marie, I was devastated, but so wanted to play that I decided to take it to the next level. It took a lot of nerve for a bashful boy to knock on the door of the Sisters' convent and ask to speak to the principal. Sister Mary Gladys. She also denied my request, but her reason had to do with authority. "I cannot overrule Sister Rita Marie without further consequences." There was a hint of want and approval in her smile and an imagined wink of her eye. I felt torn and disappointed once more. Time was running short as we were prepared to travel soon. The mode of travel was an ancient farm pickup truck with all players occupying the back with stock racks and Sister Gladys riding in front with an alumni driver.

As I returned from the convent, I encountered this "ball bus" loading for the game. One by one, players jumped on the truck with worn out baseball gloves in their hand. I walked very near to it with my heart in my hand, waiting. One of the older boys was last and asked if I was coming along. All I could do was shrug my shoulders. Roger grabbed my waiting hand and said: "Come on, let's go, we need you." The worry of what I just did was soon replaced by the excitement of a team ready to go to battle our neighbor and the hope of arriving safely in such a scary ride. We arrived safely and apprehensive as we approached their field, right next to the school and cemetery. Their umpire was the parish priest, Father Dietz.

The game started and most of the innings were, and are still a blur. I had a purpose and a job to do and I did my best. I loved it. There I was, a skinny little kid weighing 80 pounds with just a first baseman mitt and only a mask for protection, playing comparable giants in a game of equals. The game went back and forth until the late innings when our pitcher, Leon, delivered the game winning home run.

The umpire, Father Dietz, stood behind the pitcher so he could call every pitch as well as making all calls on the bases. One inning, when Leon was tossing warm-ups, father asked him: "Who is that little catcher?" Leon proudly told him: "That's my brother." Now, Father didn't know either one of us any better, because no one told him our last name was Sigwarth."

We returned home to school very happy and pleased with our victory; even Sister Gladys showed her pleasure. But I faced a punishment for disobeying authority. I had to apologize to my classmates, who were also happy for what we did. I also had to write a 500 word essay about North American Indians. What did that have to do with anything? I'll never know. In addition, I was kept from the playground during recess and noon hour for a full week.

38

I was wrong in rules and right about passion. This is a very mixed lesson about life. But I have no regrets because if things were different, I wouldn't have this story to share.

Big Brother Leon

A Good Student

It was the first day of school, and the first grade teacher decided to see how much her students knew about math.
"Mickey, can you tell me what is three and two?"
Mickey said, "That's when you should watch very, very carefully before you swing at the next pitch, but don't strike out."

Anonymous

"Small boys become big men through the influence of big men who care about small boys."

Author Unknown

FARLEY STALWART

Paul Scherrman has been involved with baseball for over a half century, as a player and manager of the Farley, Iowa town baseball team. He and his son operate the JB Scherrman Implement Company in Farley and Dyersville. He is a member of the Dubuque County Hall of Fame.

My love of baseball started at a very early age, mainly because of my dad. He loved baseball and had a real passion for the game. He wanted me to be a baseball player. I started collecting baseball cards and keeping scrapbooks when I was in early elementary school. I nailed a five gallon bucket to the garage and would try to throw baseballs into the bucket to improve my control. We would hit rubber balls before school; if you hit it so far it was a base hit, if you hit it into the neighbor's yard it was a double, and if you hit it over the street it was a homerun, that sort of thing. We only lived two blocks from the baseball field so in the summer months we would start playing about ten o'clock, come home for lunch, go back at one o'clock and at four o'clock the game was over, and the score would be like 35-28 or something.

In 1959 Dad organized the first Farley Little League team when I was eleven years old. I was the catcher and one of the youngest on the team. The pitcher was four years older and when we won the tournament I was so happy. I continued to keep scrapbooks and read everything about baseball that I could. When I was twelve, I started attending the Mickey Owen Baseball School in Moreland, Missouri. I would have to say that is where I really learned baseball. We had drills all day, and at night we would play outside teams. I remember sitting in the dugout and Mickey Owen saying, "All right, we're going to play major league rules." As a twelve year old, just the perception that "Jeez we're going to play major league rules" was really something. I went there for about four or five summers, and the last couple of summers I worked maintaining the fields to help pay for my tuition.

I went to Campion High School in Prairie du Chien, Wisconsin and in my senior year we went to the state finals. We lost the first game but two players signed professional contracts, one in baseball and another in football. Then I went to St. Mary's College in Winona, Minnesota. I caught every game my freshman year and for some reason, I thought I should play Division I baseball. Dad and I talked to a scout and he thought I should go to Bradley University. I didn't like it there so I transferred back to St. Mary's. They had a catcher there so I played in the outfield. My senior year we had a 19-2 record and on our spring trip we beat the University of Illinois two out of three.

In the summer of 1971, while playing for the Farley team, a scout from the Washington Senators said he wanted to sign me but there would be no bonus. I said: "I don't care. All I want to do is play baseball. So I went to North Carolina and played the last part of the season. The next year I went to spring training and got released. I was married with a new baby so it wasn't that big a deal. But I had realized my goal of playing professional baseball. A coach by the name of Rich Donnelly told me: "Whatever you do, don't quit playing baseball, because you can have so much fun." I remember that made an impression on me that he thought I was good enough to continue to playing, even if it wasn't at the professional level.

So I started playing for Farley in the league and tournaments and continued until I was 53. I always caught because I was a liability anywhere else. Our best year was 1987 or 1988 where we were 54-6. I caught every game.

As far as stories, there are tons of them but not all you can put in this book. One time we were playing at Miles and the batter hit a line shot that hit the pitching rubber and caromed directly back to me and I threw the guy out at first. In the late 1970's or early 80's we were playing at Placid where there was a big creek below the bank of left field. There was no fence out there so the ground rule was that any ball in the creek was in play. Our leftfielder, Don Till, had the habit of placing a warm-up ball just over the bank out of sight. One day, a Placid player hit one in the creek and I could see the splash from my view behind the plate. In just seconds, all of a sudden a dry ball is thrown back into the infield and the umpires didn't know the difference. I don't remember what happened after that because I was just laughing my head off.

We didn't always have the best umpires for these games. Even today, the umpires don't get paid enough for the grief they have to take. One day we're playing at Pleasant Grove and for some reason I was playing second base that day. The batter hits a ball down the left field line and my job as a second baseman is to watch the runner tag the base as he's rounding it. I look at the umpires as the batter rounds first and I could see they were following the ball down the left field line and not watching him tag first. Anyway the runner hits second base right on top of the bag and goes to third for a triple. I call time and tell our pitcher: "Step on the rubber to put the ball in play and throw me the ball because the runner missed second base." The pitcher asked me if the umpires saw it and I said: "He better have seen it because it would be the first thing he saw all day." The pitcher threw me the ball at second base and the umpire called the guy out.

Another time we were playing in Dubuque and there were two brothers umpiring. They were really past their prime. To put it bluntly they weren't very good. The game started and two pitches were thrown and the base umpire calls time. His brother, the plate umpire, had forgotten to put on his mask.

I remember that Pleasant Grove played on a field where there were cattle running on it during the week. They would try to clear the manure from the infield but would not always get all of it in the outfield. Also, the grass used to get 4-5 inches high in the outfield. One day the ball gets lost in the grass between the infield and out-field and it just died. Nobody could find it even though the shortstop was pretending he knew where it was. The batter rounds first and I tell him to go to second. I'm coaching third and I tell him to come to third even if he is going to be out. He comes to third and heads for home before they finally found the ball.

One time we were playing in the finals of the Worthington Tournament and we hired a pitcher from Waterloo. He was a real hit with the Farley fans because we won the game. They were giving him so much for each strike out and I think he ended up with more money from that than the $25 we paid him. A few years later, we're playing at the Anamosa Reformatory and here he shows up as an inmate pitching for the Reformatory. He had gotten into trouble for burglary.

Of course, there used to be a lot of hired guns in those days, especially for pitchers. We used to bring in pitchers from Milwaukee. They would stay at my house. It wasn't so much the money that was important to us. We just wanted to win the tournament. When there was a big game coming up people around town would ask if we were going to bring in somebody. They would even offer to throw in some of their own money. That happened more than a few times. Ed Sawville was one of the best around. He pitched for a lot of teams because he was very good. But there was one night in Worthington when he pitched for us and Holy Cross just lit him up. That was in the 80s when Holy Cross had those good teams and they beat us 10-0. He went on to pitch for a long time, even playing in the Senior League Circuit in Arizona and Florida, where I also played for about ten years. One time he was playing for a Kansas City team in the Arizona Senior League and he called me because Kansas City had lost their catcher. He said the sponsor was willing to pay for my entire trip, air fare, hotel, per diem and a car. So naturally I went.

One of the best pitchers around here in the 80's was John Ackerman from Cassville, Wisconsin. He pitched a lot of games for us and was just dominant. Another guy that comes to mind was Dave Flattery who pitched one year for Dyersville. He had pitched Triple A ball. The ball just exploded and was on you in a second. Since he played only a short time, not too many people saw him.

My managing career started in the early 70s and I'm still managing today. A highlight for me was when I was able to play in the same lineup with my three sons for a couple of years. We also went to Arizona together one year and played in a father-son tournament. Mike and I also went to play in a father-son tournament in Minnesota one year and ended up winning the tournament.

The thing about playing baseball all those years you develop a common bond with people. I was one of the players in the *Field of Dreams* movie. Hank Lucas was also one of the players. Hank and I were very competitive and intense during our playing days. Farley and Holy Cross always had a fierce rivalry. There were some incidents over the years that involved jawing and some obscenities between us. But during the *Field of Dreams* movie filming, we were teammates and all was forgotten. That's what baseball does.

"If you believe your catcher is intelligent and you know that he has considerable experience, it is a good thing to leave the game entirely in his hands."

Bob Feller

LOST NATION LAD FINDS
HIS WAY TO THE BIG LEAGUES

Jim McAndrew is a native of Lost Nation, Iowa. He graduated from the University of Iowa where he lettered in baseball. Drafted by the the New York Mets in 1965 he pitched in the big leagues for seven years. He and his wife, Lynn, reside in Fountain Hills, Arizona.

I grew up on the family farm in Lost Nation, Iowa. From the time I was five years old my older cousins and I would play baseball all the time, like work-up and that sort of thing. For me, it was a form of peer acceptance being able to tag along with the older guys. I didn't know it at the time but I guess I showed some physical ability then. I was real lucky being able to play so much, with my dad working hard on the farm trying to make ends meet. My Uncle Paul told me that dad was always a wannabe and really loved the game.

When I was about nine years old a guy by the name of Chuck Bush went to the Lost Nation Booster Club and they sponsored us by buying equipment, caps and T-shirts with Lost Nation on them. We went around to all the little towns nearby and played teams like Calamus, Wilton Junction, Clarence, Durant and Lowden. The next year we got real sophisticated and went to play in an organized Little League in the Maquoketa area. Here we were a bunch of rag tag kids playing against teams that had nice uniforms and everything and we would kick the crap out of them. It made us realize: "Hey we can play."

Starting high school, I was the smallest kid in my class, boy or girl. I was barely five feet tall. People would laugh at me being such a little guy on the mound throwing from 60 feet away. Even though we only played about 20 or 25 games in the spring and summer, I did get some exposure. So after my senior year, Larry Stolte, long time player and manager for Lowden, told my dad that he wanted me to play for his town team, since Lost Nation did not have a team. I remember one incident there that always stayed with me. I was only 17 years old and pitching for Lowden against Dixon. We faced Dick Hoeksema, a very good pitcher who had played professional ball. We lost the game in the last inning and I was tired and disgusted the way it ended. As I walked off the field I threw my glove over the dugout into the stands where my dad was sitting. As we left the park he grabbed me by the neck and said that if I ever did that again, I would never play another game of baseball. It was a very good lesson that taught me that you just don't do things that way.

About that same time, Kenny Blackman from Oxford Junction, asked my dad if I was interested in going to the University of Iowa. I had been considering one of the smaller schools like Cornell, Coe, Loras or St. Ambrose because I was a pretty decent basketball player and thought I could play both sports at one of those schools. So I called Otto Vogel at Iowa and he offered me a baseball scholarship. That's how I ended up going to Iowa. I got some coaching there and started to become a pitcher. In those days, freshmen could not compete so I did not pitch in the Big Ten my first year, but I did return to pitch for Lowden that summer.

Sometime in July of that year, 1962, a guy drove into our yard and Dad came in the house and said I'd be pitching for Rickardsville in the Cascade Tournament. I have no idea how that connection was made. So my Dad and I drove up to Cascade and when we pulled in, I thought it was a county fair because of the large crowd. In the Corn Belt League along Highway 30, we weren't used to that many people attending a game. Since it was Cascade's tournament, they thought they had paired themselves with a patsy for the first game. We surprised everyone by winning 1-0. They had a hired pitcher from Wisconsin who could really throw and he threw sort of sidearm. Anyway, I ruined the tournament for them because I got the hit that scored the only run. There was a runner on first and I was batting. I was never much of a hitter, but he threw an inside fastball that I fought off while bailing out and dumped the ball down the right field foul line, scoring the runner from first. That ruined the tournament for them and no one up there liked me very much.

Shortly after that I pitched for Earlville in the Dyersville Tournament and we won the first game. Again, I don't know how the connection was made. They thought I could really play and put me at shortstop for the second game. I was so nervous because I wasn't really a shortstop, but I managed to get through the game even though we lost.

From a father-son relationship, making those trips with my Dad to Cascade and Dyersville was very special. My old man never gave me much positive feedback, but I could just see it in his eyes how happy he was that I could play sports like that.

Sometime that same summer, Dad told me that Tom Jenk said that I was going to play for Dyersville the next year. Tom was always trying to beef up his pitching. Of course, with Art Huinker he had such a "reliable everything". He could go to the outfield and he was the best outfielder you had, and then go to the mound and again, he wouldn't blow people away but he threw strikes, he was left handed and he knew how to pitch.

When playing for Lowden I was lucky because they had an older catcher, Buzzy Benhart. He knew a little about the game and worked with me, got me to throw strikes and think out there. Then when I went to Dyersville that next year, 1963, Dale Digman was the catcher. Dale made me a pitcher. They had a good enough team up there and they worked with me so by the end of the summer I was literally a pitcher. I wasn't just a thrower anymore. I had a fastball and curve ball that I could throw for strikes. I was so proud of myself.

Dyersville was the host team for the regional ABC Tournament. I pitched a no-hitter against New Hampton the first game. They had Duane Josephson catching and Dave Wolfe was also playing for them. Dave was from Lost Nation and is my cousin. I always looked up to him because he was a good guy and a good athlete. Dave was older than me but I remember how hard he could throw. The problem was he needed more than a catcher for a target; he needed a backstop! Art Huinker won the second game and a day or so later we were playing a North Dakota team. Our starting pitcher couldn't

49

get anybody out and we had fallen behind 3-0 in the first inning. Tom Jenk came over to me and asked, "Do you think you can throw tonight?" Here I am at that young age and I said, "Sure, I'll try." I threw a few warm-up pitches, came in and struck out the side. I had better stuff than the first night. I ended up striking out 21, gave up two hits, and walked three. I mean I had outstanding stuff that night against a pretty good team.

Then when we went to Battle Creek, Michigan for the nationals I was ineffective. In fact I was terrible! I never bounced back from those two games I threw close together in the regionals. Besides, I was basically a hot weather pitcher, and in Michigan the temperature was 37 degrees. I lost the first game and really felt like I let the team down. It was the only game I lost all summer.

That fall of 1963 I went back to Iowa and pitched against the varsity lineup during fall practice. I pitched three innings, struck out eight and the other guy popped to the catcher. I had matured and basically gotten that much better because of Dale Digman and Art Huinker and the guys I played with that summer in Dyersville. I gained some confidence, got a little bit stronger and things just started falling into place. Then I hurt myself throwing too much in the field house and threw out my elbow. So I lost all of the 1964 season but the Dodgers still thought enough of me and sent me to the Basin League, but my arm still was not better. Then in my senior year, 1965, I managed to go 2-2 in the Big Ten. A scout out of St. Louis, Charlie Frye saw me pitch against Steve Arlin, a first round draft pick out of Ohio State. We lost 2-0 but he thought I deserved a chance and the Mets signed me. I pitched the last part of that 1965 season with a bad elbow and in 1966 and 1967 pitched with a crippled arm so to speak. Then in the spring of 1968 something crazy happened. I hurt my arm in spring training and my elbow popped again. I was going home but instead of going home I popped it and tore the adhesions in my arm and my arm straightened out. So I went from being a good Double A pitcher to striking out over a guy an inning in Triple A. Then I went up to the Mets that July and was able to play seven years in the Big Leagues. It's a crazy world.

50

I feel very blessed for having the opportunity to play professional baseball for all those years, especially when the first scout I ever talked to told me I was too small and didn't throw hard enough. I will always be grateful to Bob Scheffing and Whitey Herzog when I was in the minor leagues with the Mets. They showed confidence in me and were honest in giving constructive criticism. They were good communicators. My manager with the Mets for four years, Gil Hodges, was also a special man. He died suddenly in spring training in 1972. He was a gentleman and a man's man. You can go back to the Gary Cooper days and that was Gil. He didn't say much but when the veins started bulging in his neck and forehead, you knew that the volcano was about to erupt. He only did that a couple of times a year. He was a manager of men, literally. Those of us in the pitching rotation would be sitting on the bench and we could see that he was always three steps ahead of the other manager. He really was.

Baseball has been good to me. Even with my professional career, I still relish those days having one on one times with my dad as we went to those semi-pro games in Lowden, Cascade and Dyersville.

"*I became a pitcher when I stopped trying to make them miss the ball and started trying to make them hit it.*"

Sandy Koufax

TOO MUCH PEPSI-COLA

Msgr. Wayne Ressler (Ret.) is a native of Cascade, Iowa and a graduate of Loras College where he lettered four years in baseball. After seminary training and or-dination to the priesthood in Rome, Italy he returned to the Dubuqueland area and served as a priest for the Archdiocese of Dubuque until his retirement in 2011.

*G*rowing up in Cascade in the forties and fifties was a lot of fun. Baseball was "king" as far as sports were concerned. After all, Cascade was the home of Urban "Red" Faber, Hall of Fame pitcher for the Chicago White Sox. He pitched for 20 major league seasons and all were with the White Sox. He pitched in 669 regular season games and played in decades before pitch counts and relief special-ists infiltrated the game. Faber posted complete games in 56% of 483 starts. Many experts say and wrote that he was the American League's best pitcher in the early 1920s. He was inducted to Coo-perstown, New York in 1964. He had competed against nearly three dozen Hall of Famers.

So, to grow up and play for a town with as much baseball his-tory as Cascade was really exciting. The town team was called "The Cascade Reds" named after Urban "Red" Faber. There was a ritual that traditionally emerged in Cascade among the young boy baseball enthusiast. You began with picking up pop bottles at the baseball park during the game. If you could fill a pop case of used bottles and return the case to the beer stand you were paid twenty five cents.

Next you progressed to being a foul ball chaser. When players hit foul balls into the stands, parking lots or fields surrounding the park, the ball chasers retrieved the baseballs and took them to the announcing booth behind home plate where you got five cents a ball.

The next step was a big jump—sitting on the official score board sign and keeping an accurate count of the hits, runs, errors, and score for each of the nine innings. Even if it was raining and the game was not .called or delayed, the score board boys had to be on duty. That job paid twenty five cents.

Finally, the big deal was to graduate to being a team batboy. To sit on the bench with the adult players, get on the playing field to retrieve bats, rack them, and take care of the catcher's equipment after the game. If you were lucky enough to actually wear a mini team uniform, you had arrived. There was no set salary for batboys, but many of the players would tip you and buy you a pop after the game. You usually had your photo taken in the team picture which often went into the tournament information sold during pre game admission at the ball park entrances.

I actually started playing for the Cascade Reds as a 15 year old high school sophomore in 1954 and continued until I went to Rome for seminary training in 1961 I also played for the Dyersville Flyers during those years. At that time, Dyersville had two town teams, the Flyers and the Whitehawks. I even played for Balltown on Sundays a couple of years. After returning to Dubuque as an ordained priest in 1965, I played off and on with Cascade for another ten years or so.

One of my most memorable games was with Balltown on a hot July Sunday afternoon. Balltown was playing Sherrill and the manager, Earl Rettenmeier, asked me to pitch. Remember the old heavy wool suits we wore in those days. When you got heated up and began to sweat, the wool suit absorbed so much water and sweat, it felt like you were dragging another 25 pounds along with you. There was no water fountain at the ball diamond in Balltown behind Breitbach's Tavern and Restaurant. So in order to quench your thirst, you went over to a big cream can filled with water at the end of the players' bench. When I took the lid off the cream can, there was a tin ladle hanging there and I noticed at least 8 to 10 horse flies floating on top of the water in the cream can. My stomach growled, I almost up-chucked, and put the lid back on the cream can.

54

I pitched the entire game without a drink of water. About the seventh inning I began to get dizzy and I was on the verge of dehydration. I can't remember who won the game but I especially remember the post party after the game. The whole team sat under three big oak trees behind Breitbach's and the manager brought out a couple of cases of beer to quench our thirst. Since I was in minor seminary at Loras College in Dubuque, I didn't drink beer so they brought out a case of Pepsi Cola for me. I know I drank 12 to15 bottles of that case trying to quench my thirst before heading back to Cascade. About 20 minutes into the drive I had to pull over and get out of the car, I was so sick. Right on that county road, I barfed my insides out into the side ditch, for about 10 minutes. When I got home about 25 minutes later my mother said I didn't look very well. I was pale, had a fever, and felt sick. It took a couple of hours and some water, salt, and rest to recover. I never did like Pepsi Cola after that. I should have drunk the beer with the rest of the team.

Mr. Cub, Ernie Banks used to say, "It's a great day, let's play two!" That was one day I would not have wanted to play two.

"God, I just love to play baseball."
(Robert Redford in *The Natural*, 1988)

Bob Donovan, bottom row, second from left.

BERNARD TRADITION

Bob Donovan is a native of Bernard, Iowa and has been a Dubuque resident since graduating from Loras College. Bob has been in the banking business all of his adult life.

*O*ver the years, baseball in Bernard has been a fundamental social structure. They've always had a town team and are still going today. My father, Ray, was big on baseball and that's how I became interested. He played and also coached our Little League team. In fact, he is in the Dubuque County Baseball Hall of Fame.

At an early age I would go to the Prairie League games and chase foul balls, and eventually became a bat boy. Then in my senior year of high school I started to play for the town team. That was in 1968. I played about ten years until 1978 when my son was born and I decided to quit playing because of all the time away from home.

We did not have very much success early on but then started winning in the mid 1970s as we got into more tournaments. In fact, we won the Dyersville Tournament in 1975. It was a lot more fun winning. There were some guys from Fillmore that came to play for us along with Mike Weeber, a pitcher from Dubuque. He pitched for Loras and also the Dubuque minor league team. He was just tremendous and really helped us.

A funny story I remember was in 1975 when we were playing in the Lowden tournament. My wife and I had just gotten married. In the ninth inning I tried to break up a double play which I did successfully. But the next guy made out so it didn't make any difference. Anyway, I felt a pain in my side so we drank beer all the way back to Bernard. When I got home I started passing blood and had to spend a week in the hospital. My wife wasn't very sympathetic.

One year I skipped work to play on a Friday afternoon in the state tournament in Madison. I didn't do anything special that day, but I happened to score the third run of the game. We won 8-2 and the next day in the Telegraph-Herald the headline said Bob Donavan scored the winning run. After my co-workers saw that they knew I had taken off work to play ball. So I got caught.

Some of the good players I remember were the Simons from Cascade, Jerry Roling and Hank Lucas from Holy Cross, Dick Wold, Kurt Wedewer, Paul Scherman, Judd Driscoll and many others. Of course, Dyersville always had good teams and Holy Cross was really tough for a number of years. Art Huinker no-hit us in the Dyersville Tournament the last year he played. Tom Jenk hit a homerun over my head in dead center when he was at least 40 years old.

During those years I played for both Bernard and a team in Dubuque. Sometimes we would be playing with each other and the next night we would play against each other. My wife said my baseball uniforms were my main wardrobe because I wore them more than any other clothes. But it was fun. Playing with many different guys and becoming part of a team was very important. You learn to get along and that is still paying dividends today. I frequently play golf now and have a group of guys I hang around with and it is the same as when I was playing baseball.

"You have to have a lot of little boy in you to play baseball for a living."

Roy Campanella

THERE'S A SHERIFF IN TOWN

Leo Kennedy is a native of Pleasant Grove, Iowa. He worked in the peace officer field most of his adult life, serving as Dubuque County Sheriff from 1981 to 2004.

I got interested in baseball because my father played and then he later became an umpire. In fact, he umpired at the Dyersville Tournament in the early years after that tournament started around 1950.

The Pleasant Grove baseball diamond goes back to the mid 1880s. It was about as original as they come. It was in a cow pasture with a creek running along left field. Down the left field line the creek was about 250 feet to the edge of the water. The creek gave the home team a definite advantage in that the Pleasant Grove fielder would go right into the water to get a ball. If the leftfielder was standing in the water he could not see the infield, so the centerfielder would run over to the creek bank and relay the ball back to the infield, holding the runner to a double or maybe a triple. But if a Pleasant Grove batter hit the ball into the creek it was usually a home run because opposing left fielders wouldn't go into the creek.

On Sunday mornings of all home games they would drag the diamond and clean off the cow manure from the skinned infield. But they couldn't get all the manure off the grass outfield. Irwin McDermott's family still owns the property and he remembers going to ball games there when he was just a youngster. That diamond is still being used but has been fenced in, to keep the cattle from getting on the field. However, a big rainfall flooded the field a year ago so it is now in the process of being restored.

The team had good success in the 1940s and again in the 1960s when I played. We played in a lot of tournaments. In fact, we won

59

the Cascade Tournament in both 1962 and 1963. Of course, Dyersville was always tough in those days. Our team was made up of local guys like McDermotts, Thens, Simons, and Tills among others. In the tournaments we usually brought in good pitchers along with Bob Decker, a catcher from Winthrop. Some of the good pitchers were Roger Shelby, Roger Fenwick and Jim Dinger. We always had a good defensive team but our hitting was only average. There was one tournament in Worthington during that time where we took third place and scored only four runs. All the games were 1-0—we won three of them and lost the other in the semi-finals. In 1968 I had to quit playing because of my work, and the team gradually split apart.

One game stands out in my memory because of the weird things that happened on only one pitch. It was in the championship game of the Prairie League in Cascade sometime in the 60s-I don't remember the exact year. Anyway we're playing down at Cascade. I was batting with the bases loaded. On about the second or third pitch, the ball gets past the catcher and rolls back to the screen-there was a pretty good distance between home plate and the screen down there. The catcher picks up the ball and throws it to the pitcher covering home plate while the runner was sliding in. The ball gets by the pitcher and rolls back over the mound and stops a short distance behind the mound. The shortstop and second baseman come running in while the guy who was on second is rounding third and heading for home. One of the fielders picks up the ball and throws to the plate where the pitcher was still covering. Well the throw gets by him again and rolls all the way back to the screen again. When it was all over, the guy from first also scored so we scored all three base runners while I'm standing at home plate. Then I struck out. Our manager was Dan Irvin then and I told him I should get three RBIs for all that. But he didn't think so.

Another funny thing happened at Pleasant Grove one day. Instead of a pitching rubber there was a 2x6 board that was spiked into the mound. The batter hits a hard ground ball that went under the pitcher's glove and hit the 2x6. The ball went straight up in the air, at least 50 feet high. The pitcher has no idea where the ball is and he's going crazy looking around, trying to find it. Meanwhile the shortstop and third baseman are running toward the mound because they could see the ball but couldn't reach it. The ball ended up dropping right behind the pitcher. Of course the runner was safe at first.

These are just some of the crazy things you remember. Baseball is still a big interest of mine.

> *"Good pitching will always stop good hitting, and vice- versa."*
> Casey Stengel

A TRUE BASEBALL CONTRIBUTOR

Jerry Vassen is a native of Sinsinawa, Wisconsin. He has operated his own tax accounting firm in East Dubuque, Illinois for over 50 years.

*B*aseball has been a big part of my life for many years even though I never played very much. I was born and raised on a farm and we never had the opportunity to play organized baseball. I did not play high school or college ball. Our activity on the farm those days was called work. We went to school, came home and worked, and the next day we would do the same thing all over. Our dad would get mad at us if we played catch in the field in the dark at night. He thought it was a waste of time. I did play a little for East Dubuque, but only as a fill-in if they were short of players. So I became more of an organizer than a player.

From 1962 to 1976 I organized, managed, and played for the East Dubuque Sheehans. We played in the Tri-County League in Wisconsin, consisting of Kieler, Shullsburg, Benton, Belmont, Hazel Green, Galena, Dubuque, Lancaster and Platteville. We were always competitive and won a number of league championships. Bill Burbach, who later pitched for the New York Yankees, pitched for Hazel Green.

About the same time, in 1963, I organized and managed the St. Mary's Holy Name team for youngsters 14-19. We played in the Dubuque Holy Name League until 1971. Then I became supervisor for the East Dubuque Little League program, 14 and under and 12 and under and did that for 20 years until 1971. One year we had 28 teams and 44 coaches. We took those teams to the Lacrosse Stars Of Tomorrow Tournament about 50 times. Sometimes there were as many as 125 teams in that one tournament. We always played competitively and won the 12 and under open division in1984, with Pat Monahan as the winning pitcher.

Then in 1976 I organized the first boys' baseball tournament in East Dubuque for 14, 12, 10 and under teams. I ran that tournament for 15 years. One year we had 48 teams, three divisions and five fields where we played on weekends. I took care of all the maintenance. It seemed like I was dragging the fields all the time, going round and round, and round. We had many people working - umpiring, field supervisor, gates, concessions etc. It was the best tournament in the area.

During this time, 1976 to 1972 semi-pro baseball came and went in East Dubuque. In 1992, with my son Tom, we formed the East Dubuque Merchants. We played on the high school field for a number of years but it was not maintained during the summer except what I did. For the past ten years, we play our home games at Petrakis Park in Dubuque. Tom managed the team for five years and then Pat Monahan took over and has been managing ever since. Our Merchants team has done pretty well during that time. We have won our share of tournaments and had a 35 game winning streak during a period in the years 2008-10. I have coached third base all that time and plan on doing it again this year. So I've been involved in baseball over 50 years at various levels from Pee Wee to Semi-Pro.

A funny story I remember occurred some years ago in Belmont, Wisconsin. Pat Monahan's father, we called him Monk, was pitching for us against Belmont. He was a very competitive guy and started jawing with the umpire over balls and strikes. Finally, the umpire throws him out of the game. Monk said: "I'm not going". They kept arguing back and forth and Monk still refused to go. He said: "You can't throw me out; I'm just going to keep pitching." So finally, the umpire said, "Oh okay." And Monk continues to stay in the game and keep pitching. So he was thrown out of the game but he wasn't actually thrown out. We still kid Monk about that today.

Some of the top players over the years included: Pat Weber, Tim Felderman, Ray Cavanaugh, Joe Lange, Cory Schultz Mike Greibel, Frank Dardis, Paul Schermann, and Mark Pins, among others. Cascade had had many good players and they have been the top team in the area for quite awhile.

A highlight I will always remember occurred on my 70th birthday. Our East Dubuque team beat Cascade in the semi-final game of the Prairie League Championship at a 1:00 o'clock game and then went to the Peosta Tournament and beat Cascade 2-1 in a 7 o'clock game. Cascade seldom lost in those days. My youngest son, Scott, was the winning pitcher in the first game. We have five sons and all of them played baseball. From 1992-97, four of them played the infield - Tom at first base, Scott at second, Mike at shortstop, and Dave at third. Ron played in the outfield a number of years.

I want to be around the game as long as I can.

Is this a record? Tim Felderman, baseball coach at Senior High School in Dubuque, pitched a seven inning perfect game (against East Dubuque), shot a hole in one and bowled a perfect 300 game in the course of four years, 1999-2002.

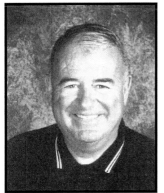

STRONG ARM- BAD JUDGMENT

Dave Wolfe is a native of Lost Nation, Iowa. He has taught high school mathematics for 45 years. He still teaches advanced math at Pleasant Valley High School in Davenport, Iowa. He also assists in coaching baseball and basketball.

My earliest memory is standing on the back side of the big barn on our farm while my two older brothers took batting practice on the other side. My job was to make sure if one of them hit it over the barn, our one and only ball would not be lost. As my younger brother, Rich and I got older we four Wolfe boys took so much batting practice against the barn that our Dad had to replace the whole side of that barn when the last Wolfe boy left the farm. We all wanted to be major leaguers. I also remember playing burn-out with my two older brothers. They were big husky guys and good athletes. I was just a scrawny younger brother and my hand would burn for hours after we finished but I was too proud to let them know it.

I thought I was a pretty good baseball player when I got to college. I did not get to play much my first two years at Loras College because of the strong lettermen ahead of me and I got hurt my sophomore year when I was the second string catcher. In my junior year, I thought I would finally get my chance. But Loras had a new baseball coach and he and I were like oil and water. I thought baseball should be fun but he was all business. I did a little pitching but he thought I was too wild and always showing off my arm, so in my senior year he decided to make me a right fielder. Now most baseball fans know that right field is the least desirable position on the diamond. But I was thrilled to play somewhere.

Early in the season we had a doubleheader scheduled on a Saturday at the old down town ballpark. The night before I went to a mixer at a neighboring girls college, Clarke College. I met a very cute blondie, Judi, and we had a great time dancing the night away. I told her we had a doubleheader the next day and she said she would try to make it. I didn't think she would show up because the park was a good taxicab ride away. The next day I'm playing right field and early in the game someone singled sharply to right with a runner on first. I knew I was supposed to hit the cutoff man who was standing on a line with third base. Unfortunately, I liked to show off my strong arm and decided to throw it all the way to third on a line. But the strength of my arm put the ball in the third base dugout, the dugout where our coach was standing. He called time, raged on to the field and yelled, "Wolfe, get in here." I was humiliated and as I was running off the field toward the dugout I saw the blondie from the night before just coming in to the park. I never played in the second game either, and nothing came of the relationship with the cute blonde.

Needless to say, my semi-pro experience was far more enjoyable. During an eight year period I played for a number of teams including Lowden, Lost Nation, Balltown, Dixon, Wyoming and New Hampton. Those tournament games in eastern Iowa were really fun, especially with the big crowds that were always there. My brother Rich and I tried to play every night, wherever there was a game that we could get to by hitchhiking or driving my old beat up car that I bought for $200. In fact one year Rich played 108 games. I even played one year in the Cape Cod League in Massachusetts along with Rich. It was a league sponsored by some major league clubs where they could evaluate promising talent. Both of us made the All-Star team.

One of my fondest memories was playing summer ball for a special man named Glenn "Shifty" Davis when I was in my teens. Without Shifty there would have been no summer ball for young kids in the area. He and another young man named Jack Marlow would drive us all over, mostly playing in the area's bigger cities. We practiced on Thursdays and played a doubleheader on Sundays. One of Shifty's favorite sayings was, "Shake it off". He never ranted or raved. If someone struck out or made an error, Shifty simply said: "Shake it off". That philosophy has stayed with me throughout life. I still help coach sophomore baseball and a few years ago I heard one of our players yell out after a bad play, "Shake it off". I smiled to myself, knowing Shifty is still with us as well as the hundreds of ballplayers who also carried that philosophy throughout their lives and taught it to others. Shifty never gave a sermon or talked about giving of yourself and your time, but he surely lived it in a big way.

"I made a wrong mistake."	Yogi Berra

CLASSIC SMALL TOWN BASEBALL

Bob Hines is a life long resident of Monticello, Iowa. After graduating From Upper Iowa University he taught English and coached high school baseball for a combined 35 years at Anamosa and Monticello. He played 31 years of semi-pro baseball for the Monticello Cubs.

We all grew up in the fifties in an era when you started playing baseball on the sandlots. We had no coaches, no uniforms, and no parents there to watch us play. My good friend, Rick Westhoff, later called it "the purest form of baseball". We didn't get our first uniform until we got to high school, and when you put on your first Monticello Cubs uniform you felt like a big leaguer. We used to get to the ball park at 6:30 for a game that started at 8:00 p.m. Our home games were on Sunday nights and we always had good crowds. There was even a large sign downtown on Main Street that said, "BASEBALL TONIGHT".

The competition in those days was fierce, but when the games were over many longtime friendships were developed. Players from other teams like Featherstone, Simon, Schnier, Roling, Stolte and many others come to mind.

It sure helped that my parents, and later my wife, Sue, were big supporters of baseball. In fact, my dad, George, played and managed for many years. Sue always said that when we were married, she got a "package deal", Bob and baseball. For years, we loaded up the station wagon and headed out to almost every ballpark from Muscatine to Holy Cross. Later, our three daughters were all queen candidates at the Dyersville tournament. Once I said I would quit baseball to spend more time at home in the summer, they all insisted that I keep playing. They knew how important baseball was to me and how much I enjoyed the game. The only thing Sue complained about was washing uniforms that had ground-in dirt and grass stains. She used to say, "Why do you have to slide and dive all the time?

Our ball park was at the fairgrounds for as long as anyone can remember. Because most residents were Chicago Cubs fans, the park was affectionately called "Wrigley Field" and the team was the Monticello Cubs. For decades, the ball field provided teams from other towns the chance to play at the Jones county Fair. The winning team got $90 and the losing team got $50. After the game, both teams joined together swapping stories and spent all of their earnings at the beer tent. Teams always wanted to be invited because it was a unique experience. The towns brought plenty of fans and they would sit under the shade trees and ate picnic lunches while watching town baseball and horse racing at the same time, since the diamond was inside the track. Sadly, that diamond was dismantled several years ago and the town games are now played at a new field in the high school sports complex.

Of course, finances were always a challenge. Mothers, daughters, wives, and girlfriends ran the concession stand. We would not have had our town team without them. We were always independent and raised our own money from the stand and donations to pay all the bills covering uniforms and equipment. We didn't have a legion, a club or even the city for financial support. It was a good year if we broke even. Al Westhoff really deserves special mention for all of his years of keeping our town team alive. He worked behind the scene many years, organizing things and taking care of the finances. It used to cost about $100 to play a home game, with the cost of umpires, balls and our old lights that were not energy efficient. The standing joke was that you'd better hustle off the field after the final out, because Al would be pulling the light switch to save on the electric bill.

During my 31 year career, I probably played 1,200 games. Most of those were with the Cubs, but I also played on occasion with Hopkinton, Muscatine and Guttenberg. I had the good fortune of playing against some great ballplayers including future major leaguers Bruce Kimm, Jim McAndrew and Mike Boddicker.

> *"I was in awe every time I stepped on to the field."*
>
> Ryne Sandberg

70

THE TENTH MAN—MR. BASEBALL
(Submitted by Bob Hines)

John Ferring was the batboy for the Monticello Cubs for 31 seasons, from 1964-1995, the same seasons I played. The first word that would come to my mind if someone asked me to describe John would be "loyal". He was loyal to his family, loyal to his friends, and loyal to his teammates.

*J*ohn was mentally challenged and lived at home with his family for all 66 years of his life. He went to our Catholic grade school through the 8th grade. He couldn't drive a car, but you always saw him riding his yellow bike. He had a job for several years at the fairgrounds horse barns, cleaning stalls and feeding the horses twice a day, year around. When I asked some longtime Cub players, nobody could ever remember when he missed a game. His big grin and good nature earned him many friends in baseball. He had a few favorite players and umpires who used to ride him good naturedly, and he'd give it right back. He had the amazing ability to remember almost every opposing player's name and number. You could ask him the name of most major leaguers and he could tell you. His favorite team was the Braves and his favorite players were Warren Spahn and Hank Aaron.

On a personal level, John and I were best friends from the time we were kids. To me he was a role model and a positive influence in my life, and for my family as well. I'd say the biggest thing he taught us was simply how to treat people. John passed away five years ago after going through some serious health problems, without ever complaining. I gave the eulogy at his funeral and the pall bearers were all former Monticello Cubs. He was buried in his uniform with his number "00" on the front.

Not a day goes by that I don't think of him, and all the fun we shared both on and off the diamond.

BATBOYS ARE IMPORTANT
(Submitted by Roger Meyer)

In my eyes, Mark Breitbach was a model batboy for the Balltown team in the fifties and sixties. I don't remember him missing a game over an eight year period, always neatly wearing his Balltown uniform.

I would sometimes use two different bats, depending on who was pitching. As I approached the on deck circle, he would have both bats there. After a short time, he would come back to the circle and ask which one I was going to use. He would then take the other bat back to the bat rack. It seemed to me he had memorized this with the whole lineup.

He never did any unnecessary talking, making my point that a batboy can play a part in the team chemistry. He did not want to interfere with the hitter's thoughts as he was preparing to hit.

When the pitcher would reach base, in an instant Mark would be on the field with his jacket. He was so efficient that he was almost taken for granted by the team.

As a coach in the Dubuque Independent League for eight years, it was very apparent to me what a good batboy means to the team.

Mark Breitbach is a graduate of Loras College. He has taught and coached at Beckman High School in Dyersville, Iowa for 37 years. He and his wife, Nancy reside in Dyersville where Mark is a member of the City Council.

QUEEN'S NIGHT

Teri Keleher was selected as tournament queen in the Farley Babe Ruth Tournament in 1985 as well as tournament queen in the 1988 Dyersville Tournament. Teri is a registered nurse and has resided with her family in Monticello for eighteen years. Her husband, Tom, owns and operates the Keleher Jewelry Store in Monticello.

*G*rowing up in Sherrill, Iowa brings back fond small town memories regarding ball, both baseball and softball. My dad was a very good left handed pitcher for the Sherrill slow pitch team. We Kress kids were drug all over northeastern Iowa to every softball diamond there was. It was funny because our mom always made sure we had a bath and looked our best before we watched Dad at his various games or tournaments. It was all for naught. We left the games with lots of dirt on us from those diamonds.

As kids we had to make our own entertainment. Since we weren't allowed to watch television during the days, we played a lot of ball. What was really neat was that Norb Kutsch had a place near Sherrill and he built a baseball field behind his house for the kids of Sherrill. He wanted to make sure that kids had a chance to play there anytime. Pick-up games by both girls and boys was a common occurrence. In my elementary school years, I also played on the Sherrill girls' team and we played against town teams like Balltown, Rickardsville, Holy Cross and Luxemburg. It was fun because everyone knew each other. Many of the other parents had gone to school with my parents.

In summertime the town baseball field was the place to be. I used to climb up the score board with local kids and we hung out there, drank our pop and ate candy bars. As I became a teenager, I would watch the boys play baseball. In 1985 Sherrill played in the Farley Babe Ruth Tournament which had a Queen Pageant. The Sherrill team selected me as their representative in the pageant. As a teenager, I was a tom boy. I liked the boys, but did not like the girlie clothes. That was a problem because each candidate had to wear a dress. Since I did not own one, I had to borrow one from an older girl. All I could say was "wow" when I was named the Tournament Queen. I went back to playing softball and watching baseball games while growing up like any other kid.

Then when I was in high school, I coached the younger Sherrill girls' team which included my sister Brenda. We won the Holy Cross Tournament one year. In 1988, the Sherrill town team selected me as their representative in the Dyersville tournament. This was special because my mother, Betty, was the queen representative for the Balltown team in 1960. People always used to say that I was the spitting image of her. So I made my way to Dyersville to meet the other candidates in all their finery. There was a nice dinner after which we were interviewed by three judges. This was intimidating but exciting at the same time. I was on the verge of leaving high school and becoming an adult. It was a great experience that helped prepare me to interview for future jobs.

The night of the pageant, I remember all the candidates sitting in the club house, looking so nervous. Between the two games, each candidate got to sit in a convertible on top of the back seat and we were promenaded all around the field, and driven to the infield. We then got out and were introduced individually. Looking into the stands with all those people, more than several thousand, was quite a thrill. It almost felt like being a rock star. Again, I was lucky enough to be selected as the Tournament Queen. It was a special evening and so much fun sharing it with my parents and future husband.

The good memories of growing up in a small town that included a lot of baseball and softball will always remain with me. I would not trade it for anything. Interestingly, organized sports has changed dramatically over the years. But I have to admit it was a whole lot easier for kids to play competitive sports then. There is so much emphasis now on AAU teams, and kids have to travel some distances and pay money in order to compete. We kept it pretty simple then, but it was a lot of fun.

Postscript: I understand Monticello's legendary batboy, John Ferring, will be included in this book.

It was my privilege to provide nursing care for John in the latter months of his illness. The first thing that impressed me about John was his smile. He grinned from ear to ear. He liked to flirt and tell stories about his glory days, hanging out with friends and the game of baseball. I really got to know him through his sister, Fran, who represented Monticello as their queen candidate one year in the Dyersville tournament.

Fran told me about John and his love of baseball, and how he played a big part in the Monticello baseball town team, as a bat boy, cheer leader, and even "statistician". She said that John loved Elvis Presley and was found dressed in his favorite Elvis costume on his birthday, sitting in the local bar, the Sports Page, where everyone came to help him celebrate his birthday. Everyone in Monticello knew who John was, and he was everybody's friend.

A record crowd of 6,389 saw the finals of the 1960 Dyersville Tournament. Independence beat Guttenberg in the championship game. Carolyn Rabe of Manchester was the Tournament Queen, Ed Watt of Dyersville was the MVP and Buzz Beatty of Dyersville received the Sportsmanship Award.

ONE OF FIFTEEN

Laurie Wessels was born and raised on a farm near Petersburg, Iowa. She has a Bachelor's Degree from Marycrest College and a Masters Degree in Business Administration from St. Ambrose College. Laurie owns and operates Wessels Group, a company that provides training and consulting services in Leadership Development. She resides in Chicago, Illinois.

* * *

Playing the game of baseball right and with proficiency is harder than it looks. In reality, baseball is a game of failure! The best hitters make out more than twice as much as they hit safely. The best pitchers lose a third of their games, sometimes because of a bad break or one bad pitch. The best baseball-minded managers often see their brilliant strategy go awry because of poor execution by players, or a wrong call by an umpire. The best umpires sometimes make a bad call, which directly changes the outcome of an important game.

That same theme is also true of queen candidates in a semi-pro tournament. Out of sixteen worthy candidates, only one walks away with the crown. The other fifteen leave with some disappointment because they were not selected. Laurie Wessels, Petersburg's queen representative in the 1980 Dyersville Tournament, has graciously shared her perspective as one of the fifteen who was not selected that year.

When I was in 2nd grade, I wanted to be on the Little League team. Instead, I was asked to be Little Miss Petersburg. A girl playing Little League was certainly not the tradition. What was tradition for girls were the baseball queen pageants. In fact I was Miss Petersburg, not once but three times – Little League, Babe Ruth and the Petersburg town team. I lost all three. How did I not learn my lesson when I was eight, I do not know. Perhaps it was the beginning of my "try it til I make it" attitude, or maybe just my ego.

I guess that even though there were very few girls to choose from, it was flattering to be asked. And I have to admit that the whole experience was both a good learning experience and also enjoyable. All the candidates got to sit in the stands with our gown and sash with the team name whenever our teams played during the tournament. It was interesting to meet the fifteen other candidates at the Queen's Dinner when we were all interviewed individually. Most of us came from small rural areas so few of us knew anyone else. I guess I should have used the phrase "world peace" when I was interviewed by the three judges. Maybe that would have made more of an impression than my stock answers to their questions.

Queen's Night itself was special. Between games each of the candidates rode in the back of a fancy convertible and we circled the entire ball park. After arriving at home plate, we were escorted to the middle of the diamond and then turned to face the large crowd of several thousand. I think all of us were nervous and excited at the same time. I even remember some of the girls were holding hands behind their back in support of each other. Not being selected as the part of the Queen's Court was definitely a disappointment. I don't recall any tears being shed, but in my own case I also was somewhat embarrassed because we then had to sit in the stands and watch the second game. The girl who was crowned Queen had the privilege of helping present the team and individual awards after the Championship Game.

Looking back, I realize that it was a very valuable experience despite not being part of the Queen's Court. As a senior in high school, it was my first opportunity to speak to a panel of judges one night and then stand in the middle of a diamond and face a large crowd on Queen's Night. It definitely helped prepare me for my subsequent professional career of providing training and giving seminars in leadership development to large business groups throughout the country.

> *"It is more admirable to compete and not "win" than not compete at all."*
>
> Anonymous

TOWN TEAM BASEBALL
MUST CONTINUE

B.J. Featherston is a native of Cascade, Iowa. Operated a tavern in Epworth, Iowa for many years before retirement. Member of Dubuque County Hall of Fame and has been the president of the organization the last four years.

I became interested in baseball at an early age, mainly because of my father. He and Red Faber, the Hall of Famer, were real good friends. My dad was a good pitcher too - he was famous for throwing the spit ball before they outlawed it. In fact he was involved in that famous 57 inning game with Ryan that went on for a couple of days. He was also inducted into the Dubuque County Baseball Hall of Fame.

When I first started high school I was a pretty good pitcher. I could really throw hard. The problem was that I was bullheaded and I overdid it. I pitched 15 innings in one day and that kind of screwed up my arm. I was also a pretty good hitter. Winky Hoerner, who managed Zwingle, was my step dad and he thought I was Babe Ruth. So he had me playing in the outfield for Zwingle when I was only 15 years old. We played in the Dyersville Tournament in 1961 and won it. I remember one tournament game in the Cascade Tournament where I played first and Neil McDermott from Epworth played short, and the other seven guys were from Parsons College when they had those good teams. Winky always had a lot of money and would get players wherever he could.

After a couple of years playing for Zwingle, Noel Callahan from Epworth talked me into playing for them, but I still continued playing for Zwingle on Sundays for a few years. So Epworth is where I played and managed until I retired in 1984. I thought it was time for somebody else to take over. But I have remained active in baseball ever since. I've had both my feet amputated, but I still try to be around the game as much as possible because I love it so much.

I hate to use the word "I" all the time but I represented the town of Epworth when they bought the land for the new ball park a number of years ago. That took a lot of time getting that ballpark built. I also started the "Over 40 League" in the early 90's, just to keep the interest going. That went over good for a few years before it kind of died. In fact, Joe Hoerner came back and played in that first game. When you talk about the Hoerners, Joe's brother Bob was the nicest guy I ever met. Being around baseball for so long, you meet a lot of good guys, but, oh man, Bob Hoerner was something else!

I really try to emphasize the Dubuque County Hall of Fame. Those of us involved with the organization remain active because we think that is one way to keep baseball alive up here. It seems like the interest just isn't there like it used to be. We are constantly thinking of ways to promote it and keep it going. There are some great ballplayers in that Hall of Fame and we don't want to water it down by electing people just for the sake of electing.

The best ballplayer that I ever saw around here was Art Huinker. He was all around - he could do it all. The best home town pitcher I ever saw was Dave Reittinger from Dyersville. They called him "Hootenaney". He had the best curve ball around.

As far as good stories I have a lot them, but none that you should probably put in this book.

"The wind always seems to be blowing against the catchers when they're running."

Yogi Berra

SECRET SIGNALS IN SHERRILL

Lenny Young was an outstanding pitcher in Dubuque's Holy Name League. He pitched for Wahlert High School and played semi-pro baseball with the Sherrill, Iowa town team. He also officiated three high school sports - football, basketball and baseball.

*I*t was in the late sixties, a beautiful Sunday afternoon in Sherrill, Iowa. The home team was hosting a Prairie league opponent. I was a 19 year old city kid asked to pitch on a team of local players from Sherrill. Teammates seemed to be mostly related, or at least close friends, but I do recall three brothers being the mainstays of the team. Jerry was the catcher, Jimmy played first base, and Albie played second.

It was the top of the first inning, and I walked the leadoff batter. Jimmy, the first baseman, called time and walked to the mound. Being a veteran of the Prairie League, Jimmy seemed to have some knowledge of our opponent's strategy. He said to me: "Lenny, I think I know their steal sign. When I see it, I'll give you a signal, and you make a pickoff move, and we'll catch him leaning the wrong way and pick him off." "Sounds good to me," I said. "What's your signal gonna be?" Jimmy hesitated a moment and whispered, "I'll say Humpty Dumpty." I said, "You sure?" "Yep," Jimmy said. "That's it," and trotted back to he first base position.

I was a little surprised at the signal, but I thought I better do what I was told to do. I toed the rubber, looked for a sign from Jerry, the catcher, who gave me two fingers indicating a curve ball. I shook him off because just in case Jimmy said, "Humpty Dumpty," I wanted a fastball grip to throw over to first. Jerry gave me one finger for the fast ball. I nodded approval, went into the stretch, hesitated, and looked over my shoulder at first. Jimmy said nothing. I looked back at my catcher's target. As I began my motion toward home plate, at the top of the extension of my right arm, I heard a loud beller from behind me, "Humpty Dumpty." It was too late. I threw the pitch about ten feet over the batter's head. The runner trotted to second base.

Between innings, Jimmy agreed we needed to change our signal. "I'll think of something," he said. So sure enough, the next inning, a runner reached first base. Jimmy called time, came to the mound, and said, "This time if the steal is on, I'll say a National League team. If the steal is not on, I'll say an American League team." I thought what the heck, at least I'll know one way or the other...he's either going or not going. As I went into my stretch, Jimmy yelled, "CHICAGO." I stopped and yelled, "CUBS or WHITE SOX?" The umpire called a balk, and the runner advanced to second base. So much for intricate signals between pitcher and his fielders in the Prairie League.

When Joe DiMaggio was asked what it was like being married to Marilyn Monroe, Joe replied, *"It beats rooming with Joe Page."*

A LONG CAREER—
AND STILL GOING

Len Tekippe grew up in Rickardsville, Iowa. He has been playing and managing the town team for over 40 years.

My Dad, Benedict, was a baseball fanatic even though he never really played. That's how I became interested in the game, just listening and going to games with him. He also started the Little League program in Rickardsville. I started playing Little League and then went on to all the other levels like Babe Ruth, Junior Legion, High School, and then the town team in 1972 when I was 17 years old. I even played for a couple of years at Loras College but I did not have a distinguished career there.

During the years I was playing and managing at Rickardsville, I also played some for Balltown, Key West, and Kieler. That was because they were all in different leagues so I played when I was available. As a result, I made a lot of good friends over the years with guys from different towns.

I'm probably one of the few guys who started out with wood bats, then went to aluminum bats, and now back to wood bats. There's quite a difference between the two, especially with the later aluminum bats. They had a lot more pop. With those bats, I hit quite a few home runs during my career, probably over 200. On four different occasions I hit three home runs in a game. One year our Rickardsville team had over 100 home runs.

I always tried to be well organized as a manager. In fact, I have most of the scorebooks from all the years I managed. We have won 40 tournaments over the years. Of course, there are a lot more tournaments now than there used to be when there were only three or four. Our best years were 1986 when we won three tournaments and had a record of 36-14, and in 1995 when we were 34-9 and also won three tournaments.

As far as individual players, several good hitters come to mind: Tom Jenk, Mick Meyer, Paul Sherrman, and Steve Kaiser. Probably the most impressive individual feat I remember is Steve Kaiser's performance in 1983. He pitched 48 innings in eight days. Only he and I knew about it because we were playing together for Keiler and Rickardsville. He pitched four complete seven inning games and 20 innings of relief. He topped it off with three innings of relief in the championship game when we beat Petersburg in their own tournament. He later went on to play fast pitch softball for a team in Cedar Rapids and they went all over the world. He still pitches baseball in old timers' games.

A couple of interesting stories. In 1979 we beat Dyersville in the semi-final game of their tournament. We hired a pitcher, Tom Klawitter, who later pitched for the Twins. In the championship game against Farley, we brought a pitcher in all the way from Arkansas who had pitched for the university in Fayetteville. Farley hit him pretty good and we got beat 9-2. Their pitcher for that game had been the number one pitcher for Iowa that spring. Fans couldn't believe that our guy had come all the way from Arkansas. So that's one decision that backfired on us.

In the 1998 Dyersville Tournament, we're playing Dyersville and the game is tied 1-1 in the 11th inning. We had a hired pitcher by the name of Kevin Benzing from Wisconsin and I went out to talk with him because they had the bases loaded and nobody out. As I came to the mound he starts using all kinds of profanity. He points to the batter and said, "I'm gonna get him and then the guy over there", pointing to the on deck circle, and "then the --- who's gonna come out of the dugout". He struck them all out.

I don't know how long I will continue managing. I'll just go from year to year, sort of like the one year contracts that Walter Alston used to have with the Dodgers.

"I was such a dangerous hitter, I got walks even in batting practice."
                                                              Casey Stengel

---

Seventh
Inning
Stretch

The Simon Nine _ Early 1900's

Nick, Joe, John, Mike, Peter, Matt, Leo, Louis, Willy

Bernard's Best - 1912

Back Row: Frank Maloy, Clarence Maloy, Willie Cannon, Joe Noonan
Front Row: Charlie Driscoll, Jerry Ryle, Joe Callahan, John Williams, Leo Donnovan

1918

The Breitbach Brothers

Noteworthy News

BASEBALL

Reformatory Greys
Vs.
Dubuque Koolmotors

The Greys have been looking like a real ball club this year in practice. From the way they are hitting the ball it looks like a far better team than last season.

Dubuque always has a good team and they are a smart bunch of ball players. You can always be assured of a good fast ball game when these two teams meet.

"CRABBY" SAVEL WILL UMPIRE

Thursday, May 30th
1:30 P.M.
AT THE REFORMATORY
Anamosa, Iowa

New Bleachers For All
Refreshments on Grounds

PUBLIC INVITED — — — — **Admission 25¢**

Estimated to be from the 1930's this clipping from the Telegraph Herald was provided by Victor Sprenglemeyer of Dubuque, Iowa.

At **Cascade Legion Park-2:30** P. M.

WORTHINGTON

Champions of Maquoketa Valley League.

VS.

KOOLMOTORS

Dubuque City Champions

The battle of the season-two Championship teams meeting for the Eastern Iowa Title. Two Clubs with Plenty of Batting Power and Two Best hurlers in this section, Krueger for Worthington and Sprenglemeyer for the Koolmotors. This is a Challenge Game, and a Battle Royal is assured.

ADMISSION--Adults, 25c.   Children, 10c

Estimated to be from the 1930's this clipping from the Telegraph Herald was provided by Victor Sprenglemeyer of Dubuque, Iowa.

Two Dubuque Hall of Famers,
brothers Jim and Paul Schmitt, Rickardsville.

May 1961

Lots of Glasses -- And Victories, Too

Pitcher Bill Diehl (left), catcher Bob Meyer (right) and the entire Loras College infield wear glasses. But their answer to any jibes is their record: 10 victories against only three losses. From left: Diehl, third baseman John Spinner; shortstop Jerry Splinter; second baseman Jack Higgins; first baseman Wayne Ressler, and Robert Meyer.

Reprinted with permission of the Des Moines Register

Splinter, Ressler and Meyer played semi-pro ball in the Dubuque area.

1963 Champs

The 1963 Great Plains Regional AABC Tournament Champs.
(L-R): Jim McAndrew, Dale Digman, Art Huniker and Tom Jenk

Jim McAndrew with Carl Erskine and Carl Furillo

1978 Dyersville Tournament - Trophy Winners

Front row: Kenny Ruden, Dave Kirsch, Rob Roling, Judd Driscoll, Jerry Roling
Back Row: Mike Koelker, Hank Lucas, Rose Link, Dennis Meloy, Dick Dupont

Grand Slam!

Bill Pins, Holy Cross left fielder, is hoisted into the air by Ron (Hank) Lucas after he hit a grand slam in the top of the ninth inning to win the Worthington Tournament, 8-6, over Farley in 1980.

MEMORIES FROM GUTTENBURG

Norb Borcherding grew up on a farm in Guttenberg, Iowa. He played baseball in high school and a few years with the Guttenberg Braves town team, and one summer with the Ft. Leonard Wood base team while serving in the National Guard. He resides in Dubuque, Iowa and has operated his own company, Double L Group, for 42 years.

I became interested in baseball at an early age, somewhere in the 1950's. My dad, Herb, was the manager of the Guttenberg Braves for at least 20 years, and I started off being batboy, and then scorekeeper. In fact, I still have a lot of the old scorebooks. My dad was also my high school teacher. Our Sunday activities revolved around baseball. We went to all the tournament games as well. A lot of the towns had tournaments during the week. Of course, Dyersville was always the big one with the queen pageant and all.

I was always a Milwaukee Braves fan. One of my favorite boyhood memories was when my dad and I went to Milwaukee to see the Braves play the San Francisco Giants. While we were watching batting practice, some media guy came and asked if we would like to be on TV. So he took us down on to the field where I got to sit between Warren Spahn and Juan Marichal. Both of them gave me their autographs. The ABC television cameras were rolling and Howard Cosell was the TV guy on the field. He asked me who I thought would win the pennant. I was so nervous sitting beside these two famous players I didn't know what to say so I said the New York Yankees. He said, "Son, I think you've got your leagues mixed up."

We also went to the Twins games in Minneapolis where I got to see Harmon Killebrew and the other great players the Twins had. At one game, they were playing the New York Yankees and Mickey Mantle was playing left field that particular game. A guy was on third base and the batter hit a fly ball toward Mantle. As the ball was going toward him, my Dad said, "Now watch a great ball player make this throw to the plate." Wouldn't you know, Mantle dropped the ball.

I joined the National Guard in the early sixties and did my active duty training at Ft. Leonard Wood, Missouri. They always had strong ball clubs. I was fortunate to make the base team as a relief pitcher even though I was only there for about three months. I thought I was pretty decent. I remember one game where I was brought in to pitch in the 9th inning with the bases loaded and nobody out. I could throw pretty hard and struck out the first two guys on six pitches. So I was feeling pretty cocky. Anyway this big clean up hitter came up and he was going through all kinds of motions— kicking dirt, digging a hole to plant his rear foot, squeezing the bat and all kinds of things. So I thought I would be real cool and step off the mound, pick up some dirt and throw it in the air behind me. Well, the wind was blowing pretty good and it blew the dirt back in my face, right into my eyes. I couldn't see so they had to take me out of the game. The pitcher who relieved me gave up a base clearing double to win the game.

I also remember pitching against Dyersville one night and Jack Dittmer was up. Of course he was a great athlete at the University of Iowa, lettering in football, basketball and baseball. They said he was never that good a hitter, but he did play for the Milwaukee Braves a number of years. Anyway, the catcher wanted me to walk him after my first two pitches were balls. I thought I could throw pretty hard and wanted to get at least one strike against my idol. So I threw a fast ball right down the middle. He hit that ball so high and far it went over the lights in right field, but he was so far out in front of it that the umpire yelled "foul ball". So I got my goal of throwing a strike against Jack Dittmer.

One night we were playing at Worthington and Joe Horner, the future major league pitcher, was pitching against us. The first pitch he threw me I never saw, but the umpire told me to take my base because he said the pitch hit me. I didn't know what happened until I looked down and the end of my belt was still moving. I was just shaking. I got to first base and thought to myself, "This is really dangerous".

Our Guttenberg team had some really good ball clubs in those years. Guys like Merle Hyde, Al Klinger, Duane Hagan, Bruce Hinkle and Rod Tangeman were great players. And those Guttenberg fans really got into it. I remember this one lady used to bring a dirty old beat up baseball with her. When a batter hit a foul ball into the stands, somebody would give her the new ball and she would throw the old beat up ball back on the field.

Of course the Dyersville Tournament was always the big draw. On Queen's Night and the finals, they would have almost 5,000 people there. Some teams would really load up and bring in some great ball players. One time, a well-to-do businessman from Guttenberg told my dad that he should get the best possible pitcher to beat Dyersville. So my dad contacted a Cincinnati scout who recommended this guy from Sun Prairie, Wisconsin. He was offered so much to win, so much if he lost and $10 for every strikeout. He was an outstanding pitcher and was striking guys out but the catcher couldn't hold him. He came to the dugout and said he couldn't see the pitches, so this pitcher had to throw nothing but straight balls. He still struck out 10 guys, but I know he could have struck out a lot more if the catcher could have held him.

Those are some of my good memories and I have many more. It's too bad that baseball doesn't have the same interest anymore. Baseball did a lot of good for a lot of people. I know there are still many town teams, but the fan interest just isn't there. I don't know what happened. I guess it's because of television and there are too many other things going on.

The following are excerpts of a letter from Helene Kuempel to her "Little Brother" Norb about their Dad, Herb.

Many years ago our Aunt Gertie Anderegg told me that Herb was an extremely bright kid who loved baseball.

I can't recall the circumstances that caused Dad to organize his own team but it was somewhere in the 1954-55 time frame. A few years after that, Dad was able to take his team into the grand daddy of area baseball tournaments at Dyersville where they proved to be competitive that first year. After that, area fans would give Dad cash to pay mileage to load up with good players for the tourneys. That is when players like Al Klinger (West Union), Ken and Keith Crider (Elgin) Howie Kettleson (Clermont) Eli Krogman (Wisconsin) Jim Borcherding (Sumner) Bob Buelow and Tom Turner (Dubuque) came on board along with some others.

Dad scanned the sport pages of the Telegraph Herald looking for his hand picked teams. He also umpired high school games which helped in his scouting.

Another neat story is that there was a little boy with a disability and a speech impediment who showed up for every game in Guttenberg. Dad and Mom took a liking to him and would always drive into town to pick him up for away games. They even bought him a baseball uniform and hat to wear. In the later years you and Milt were able to be bat boys and sit on the players' bench.

BASEBALL TRIVIA:

Hall of Famers Henry Aaron, Ernie Banks, Reggie Jackson, Willie Mays, Bill Mazeroski, Tony Perez, Willie Stargell and Carl Yaztremsiki batted 89 times against Joe Hoerner. What was their collective batting average against him?

Answer: 101

RONNIE'S BAG

Bob McCabe is a native of the Fillmore, Iowa area. He moved to New Vienna, Iowa in 1979 and still resides there. Bob has been in the banking business his entire professional career. He also participated with the <u>Field of Dreams</u> players.

At the time I moved to New Vienna in the late seventies, the town did not have a baseball team. I had been playing for Worthington ever since I got out of the military service in 1974 and continued playing for them until 1986. That's when we formed the New Vienna Stars because there was a lot of interest among many young local guys. Jerry Wessels and I started the team and I was the player manager. We had to call ourselves something so we went back in history and found out that the team had been named the Stars and Cubs at different times. We decided against the Cubs so we chose Stars as our team name.

We had a good ball club. They were all good players and good athletes. And we were all local. We were 18-0 before we got beat that first year. Our season record was like 30-5. We continued having 25-30 win seasons for quite a while. It took us three to four years before we got invited to tournaments, but we did very well once we were in them. We usually made it to the final four. We had five really good pitchers – Tom Westhoff, Glen Naber and Ron Wedewer among them. Wedewer was really good. He was probably the best ballplayer that ever came out of New Vienna; good fielder, good hitter, and a good pitcher. We continued to have local guys for several years and then later added a few others from Petersburg, like Greg Wessels. Greg was a good left-handed hitter who had some power. He was up there to hit, but he also had a very sharp eye at the plate and very seldom struck out. He was MVP in a couple of tournaments when he played here.

I managed until 1992 and then gave it up, but I continued playing until I was in my 40's. When I managed I always told those guys,

"At the time of the first pitch we have our game faces on, we're here to play baseball, we're serious, and we're here to win." That was my philosophy. I wanted them here on time and I wanted them to give a hundred percent while they're playing baseball. I told them that when the game is over, it's over and they can do what they want to do but when they're here they're serious. That was my style.

A funny story. Ron Wedewer, our good ballplayer, was single and living in the Petersburg area while he was playing for us. It never failed, almost every game he would forget something from his uniform. It might be a uniform top, bottom, leggings, belt, hat, something. So I started bringing a separate bag where I had a complete uniform in it that would have whatever he forgot. I even had a glove in it, which he forgot sometimes. The players called it "Ronnie's Bag". If anybody else forgot something, they always knew I would have something in Ronnie's bag to help them. So, in addition to carrying my own bag and the team equipment bag, I always carried an extra bag called "Ronnie's Bag."

One of my fondest memories of all my playing and managing days occurred when I was playing for Worthington in the early 80's. We were playing in the Sherrill tournament. Dubuque had a team called the Dubuque Blues and for a number of years they won the tournament. So they had to be invited back every year to defend the title. Anyway we beat them in a first round game that year. It was in extra innings and we trailed by three runs in the bottom of the tenth inning. There were two outs, bases loaded, and a three-two count on the batter, me. With everybody running I managed to hit a grand slam walk-off home run to win the game and eliminate the favorites. All the other teams around there like Rickardsville, Holy Cross and Balltown were so happy that we had finally broken the streak of the Dubuque team and now they had a chance to win the tournament. They were all buying me more beer than I could drink. That had to be the highlight of my playing career.

> *"I couldn't have done it without my players."*
>
> Casey Stengel

104

BASEBALL IN THE
"BIG HOUSE"

Dick Schnier farmed in the Worthington, Iowa area most of his life. He also worked for 20 years as a security guard at the Men's Reformatory in Anamosa, Iowa. He is a member of the Dubuque County Baseball Hall of Fame. He continues to make his home in Worthington.

I became interested in baseball at an early age because of my brother Jim who caught for the Worthington Cardinals. I began pitching in high school and started playing for the town team around my senior year. In my first year pitching semi-pro baseball I learned a valuable lesson. We were in the second round of the Cascade tournament and I was pitching. Our catcher, Dale Digman, had four years of experience behind the plate. During the first few innings I occasionally shook him off. Finally he called time, came to the mound and said in a loud voice, "don't stand out there shaking your head like an old bull, throw the -----pitch I call for." For the rest of that game and the rest of the year I threw the pitches he called. That made me realize rookies have a lot to learn.

One of my most interesting and unusual experiences in semi-pro ball was playing inside the Anamosa Reformatory in Anamosa, Iowa. The reformatory used to have a team in the Delaware County League and were even allowed to play away games outside the walls for a couple of years. But that stopped because some of the towns protested; they thought it was too dangerous.

Anyway, one Sunday afternoon in 1968 I was playing for Hopkinton and we traveled to Anamosa to play the reformatory inmates. From the outside, the prison looks like a castle that you might see in Europe. It was built in the 1800s with rock that came from a quarry in nearby Stone City. Getting inside is quite an experience. First, all of the players must all go in at the same time. They put you in a room and search everyone for contraband - knives, nail clippers, spray cans - anything that could be a danger inside. All of the equipment was searched along with the bags holding the balls and bats. After that, they put you in a small area that looks like a cage. It is called a sally port and has bars on three sides and the fourth side is a bullet proof glass that looks inside the control room. That room is manned by several security officers who control the electronic gates. When the gates slam shut, it really sounds and feels like a prison.

From there we had to go through another gate to get into the prison yard which has the ball diamond on the far end. The outfield is not enclosed by a fence, but by a 50 foot wall from the left field foul line to center field, and by a big two story rock building from centerfield to the right field foul line. On top of the wall in left centerfield, there is a guard tower with an armed security guard. That tower is manned 24 hours a day.

The ball diamond has a dirt infield that is mixed with coal cinders. The reason for the cinders is that a railroad track used to run through the outfield, bringing in coal which was used to heat the prison. Naturally, that infield caused a lot of bad hops and strawberries for players who dared to slide.

After all the players got on the field, our 20 or so fans came in and went through the same security check as the players. They were seated in the covered bleachers right behind home plate. We were batting in the third inning when two inmates came running from behind a building and onto the ball diamond. One inmate was the chasing the other with a baseball bat in his hand. The first inmate had blood all over him so he must have been hit a few times. A short distance behind were several corrections officers who chased the inmates across the diamond and behind another building. That was the last we saw of them. I suppose they were captured and placed in solitary confinement for a long time.

The game was stopped and officers escorted our team and fans outside the prison. About 45 minutes later, our team was allowed to go back inside to finish the game, but our fans had to stay outside the prison for the rest of the game.

No other semi-pro game that I played was as eventful as that one.

> *"I'm an escaped car thief. I broke out of prison to see the Cubs in the World Series."*
> James Belushi in *Taking Care of Business*, 1990.

*Mike Knake (back row, second from left) is a lifelong resident of
Bellevue, Iowa where he has farmed with his brother all his life.*

Bellevue had a town team for many years starting in the 1940's.
They were known as the Merchants until 1958 when they changed to
the Beavers for two years. In 1960 the name was changed to Braves,
the name still used today. We always had our own players so we
never won very much. Also we did not get lights until about 1985
so we never got invited to very many tournaments. However, the
team did win the Prairie League championship in 1968 and 1969.
I played for 20 years, from 1970 to 1990. I got interested in baseball because Dad played a little in his younger days and he always
encouraged my brother and me. Then I played in high school and
started with the Braves my first year after high school. We always
worked the ball games around our farm work. Larry Conrad was our
manager then and we had a couple of good years before the older
guys retired and we started all over again.

The guy who really kept baseball going in Bellevue was Tuffy
Ernst. He got his nickname when he was pretty young, like in the
1940s. He was a batboy and got hit with a ball but he never cried.
After that he was always known as Tuffy. He was involved for over
50 years, between playing and managing. Baseball was his life - the
town team and the Chicago Cubs. He was the driving force in getting lights installed in the mid eighties.

I remember a couple of funny stories involving Tuffy when I was
playing. It was a hot Sunday afternoon - we always played on Sundays. We were getting beat pretty bad and our pitcher wasn't throw-

107

ing strikes. So Tuffy goes to the mound and talks to him. When he comes back to the bench he mumbles to himself: "Our pitcher said he can't throw strikes because he has a square ball". Another hot day after we got beat pretty bad, our pitcher and catcher got into an argument. They even played basketball together in the winter. Anyway our catcher was criticizing our pitcher that he didn't throw hard that day. Our pitcher said: "Well I was throwing faster than you were running to first base." So before you knew it they lined up at home plate and sprinted down to first base. They did that three or four times. Tuffy mumbled: "I sure wish they would have put that much energy into the game today."

Our big moment of glory was in 1981 when we won our own tournament. We beat some pretty good teams along the way. We really celebrated because that was our only championship. Tuffy was so happy he was crying.

Another guy who did a lot for Bellevue baseball was Louie Jess. He was a manager and long time fan. He left money in his will which was used to start the annual Bellevue Tournament, known today as the Louie Jess Memorial Tournament.

The modern day Braves have won the Louie Jess Memorial several times. They have also won other area tournaments, including the 2011 Dyersville Tournament, a first. Like most small towns these days, there aren't as many local guys playing as there used to be. The notable Bellevue players today are the manager, Chet Knake, Mike and Willie Griebel, Pete Bonifus, Corbin Ploessel, Brad Boekenstadt, Rick Reeg, Jarrod Koos, and Jordan Ries.

Tuffy Ernst is the first baseman. The UFH (Unidentifed Flying Human) is unknown.

RECOLLECTIONS OF BASEBALL

Gene "Tiny" Potts is a graduate of Loras College where he lettered in basketball and baseball. Received his PHD in Education Administration from the University of Iowa. He spent his entire career in education, teaching and administration. Played semi-pro baseball for a number of Dubuqueland area teams over a 30 year span. Was coach for the Ghost Players in the <u>Field of Dreams</u> movie. Coached in the Dubuque Independent League, managed the Dubuque Merchants and Budweiser's semi-pro teams. Member of the Loras College Baseball Hall of Fame, Dubuque County Baseball Hall of Fame, Independent League Hall of Fame, and the Iowa AAU Athletic Hall Of Fame.

*F*rom my recollection, the semi-pro baseball players played baseball with a passion second to none. They went to great lengths to play a game. They were given the schedule and did not need to be called or reminded. Family, work, and church were the only reason to miss or be late for a game. Sometimes those responsibilities even took a back seat to a baseball game.

Many players helped prepare the infield, cut the grass, and groomed the field for play. They held fundraisers to raise the money to cover expenses of the baseball operation. One hot Sunday, we played a doubleheader in the afternoon and a nine inning game in the evening. We drove 50 miles to play nine innings in a tournament. No one complained about being tired, hot, or anything. That's the way it was – for the love of the game. There are many memorable stories:

Hot Corner Incident

"Time Out, Ump!" yelled our manager and strolled to the mound. As the infielders gathered on the mound we were all wondering why time had been called. We also wondered why our third baseman was so late arriving to the huddle. We soon got our answer. Our manager, Louie, looked at our late arrival and calmly stated, "Tuck, you're playing third base, not left field. We don't need two left fielders." Tuck replied, "Here, you play third. I don't want to get killed." He threw in a few expletives to make his point. We knew immediately why he was playing 30 feet behind third. Big John Moran was up. John, who later became Father John, was notorious for how hard he hit balls to the left side of the field, especially third base. We broke from our huddle at the mound with a better understanding why we used two left fielders that night.

Far, Far Into the Night Those Balls Flew

One night our young Dubuque Merchants team was playing against the veteran Dubuque Star Brewers at the old Fourth Street Ball Park. The dimensions of that park were long – 340 feet to right and left fields, and 410 to dead center. Our pitcher was a young fire-baller who had just finished his freshman year pitching for the University of Iowa. He threw in the nineties and had a wicked curve ball. Our young team was confident that we could beat this very good veteran team.

Our young pitcher had a difficult time finding the plate. There must have been 15 walks in that nine inning game. However, not one walk went to the best left-handed hitter in the Dubuqueland area. His first time at bat, he hit a home run to right center that went over the light tower. The second time he hit a home run, again over the tower in right center. You guessed it, the third time he hit another homerun that cleared the light tower, this time more toward center field. The fourth time he hit a major league pop-up that seemed to never come down until I caught it. As Bob Hoerner rounded second base, I asked him if he wanted the ball I just caught, since we would never find the other three. "No, Tiny," he chuckled, "You keep it. We're going to need it to finish this game."

The Tobacco Episode

Years ago many baseball players chewed tobacco. Leaf tobacco was very popular. A big cheek-full was a common sight on many a ball diamond. I never could see the benefit, but many players obviously enjoyed chewing during the game.

110

One incident that brings back a somewhat humorous memory was the time my teammate swallowed his chew as he rounded second base on a gapper. By the time he reached third, he was starting to swerve. Halfway between third and home, he was swaying as if a strong wind was pushing him sideways and back again. He looked like he was running an "S" pattern, not a straight line to home plate. He finally staggered home and headed straight behind the dugout to get rid of the cause of his problem. P.S We made sure he touched home plate before he headed behind the dugout.

Not Too Bad For One Eye

The umpire's glass eye must have been his left because he consistently missed strikes on the inner half of the plate. Our pitcher was becoming frustrated as were his teammates. We needed to do something immediately as this game was extremely important for us to advance. I, as the catcher, went to the mound and told our pitcher to throw a ball as hard as he could, and I would do the rest. The 90 plus fastball was on the inner half of the plate. At the last instant, I ducked down, and the ball made a very large thud as it hit the large balloon chest protector of old one-eye. He was pushed back and almost fell down. He ripped off his mask and let me have it. "You did that on purpose!" he said. "No, I didn't, Murph! It was on the inside corner, and I just missed one. You missed at least ten just like it tonight." He looked squarely at me and said, "Let's play ball."

As Murph leaned over me, I noticed he was a little more over my left shoulder. As I told him after the game, "It's a good umpire who makes appropriate adjustments to call a better game." The smile on his face was very telling. We remained good friends until the day he died. I know Murph is in heaven. And if there is baseball going on, he will be umpiring, and I'll bet that he is watching that inside corner.

"My mother had a great deal of trouble with me, but I think she enjoyed it"

Mark Twain

GROWING UP WITH A DREAM

Art Huinker grew up on a farm family near Festina, Iowa. He received his Bachelor's Degree from Loras College and a Doctorate in Educational Administration from the University of Illinois. Had a perfect 19-0 record in his four year career at Loras College with an ERA under 2.00. His Dyersville Beckman High School baseball team won the state championship in 1968, competing against much larger schools. Art spent his entire career in education: teaching, coaching, and administration. He is a member of the Loras College Hall of Fame, Dubuque County Baseball Hall of Fame, the Iowa High School Baseball Coaches Hall of Fame, and the Iowa High School Referees' Hall of Fame. After raising their seven children, Art and his wife, Ann, reside in Peosta, Iowa.

*G*rowing up in a rural setting and a small baseball town of Festina, Iowa, about the only sport we recognized was baseball. That was partly due to the influence of my "daddy" who wore the tools of ignorance when he was young. Baseball was his love and he supported my two brothers, Linus, Kenny, and me to play the game almost whenever we wanted to. Farm work did get in the way once in a while, but baseball was always a high priority.

After completing ten years of Catholic school education, where there were no organized sports, I became a pitcher for neighboring Calmar Public High School. We were the first team in any sport from that school to play in the semi finals where we lost to the eventual champion, Kanawha. That experience plus playing for hometown Festina, starting at age 15, landed me a scholarship to Loras College. Four years later, I pitched my last game as a senior with a record of 19-0.

The St. Louis Cardinals offered me a contract, which I accepted with a signing bonus, after I graduated from Loras. I pitched about six weeks in the summer of 1957, primarily in Albany, Georgia. I left before the season ended to fulfill a teaching contract I had signed in the spring of my senior year at Loras. It was a successful season with a 6-1 record and an ERA of 1.23. That performance gave me hope that my dream of playing professional baseball would be fulfilled. A contract was offered the following winter at Class B Winston-Salem, but it remained unsigned because the salary limitations imposed by the big leagues was so minimal that I found it impossible to meet our family's needs. End of that dream.

For the remainder of my ball playing days, hometown Festina and Dyersville, Iowa were the primary locations. I played until 1968, at the same time that my official coaching of high school baseball ended at Beckman High School. My last team won the state championship, one of the greatest rewards I ever experienced. Of course, my wife, Ann, will always be the best reward, bar none.

Invitational tournaments in the Dubuque County area are a major factor in keeping baseball so strong in this area. One of those tournaments will always remain as a great memory for me. It was in the 1956 Cascade Tournament, when I was still in college. In the four games, I pitched two no hitters and a one hitter and had a bases loaded triple in the semi final game that helped the Dyersville Whitehawks reach the championship game where I pitched one of my no hitters. This all took place a week after our first son was born. Might there be a connection?

Because two of our sons came into this world after the conclusion of my playing days, they requested that I put together a huge scrapbook of games played and accomplishments. That idea has led to the writing of a book that goes back to why baseball was so important to the Leo Huinker family, to the day when my playing and official baseball coaching ended. If I get my days organized, it should be published in the fall of this year.

> *"If you play the game of baseball, always hustle until it hurts; then you will have enjoyed the game."*
>
> Art Huinker

EL SPEEDO

Jim Wegman is a lifelong resident of Petersburg, Iowa. He has operated his own milk route business for over 50 years. Jim is a member of the Dubuque Baseball Hall of Fame.

I grew up on a farm in Petersburg. For as long as I can remember, we farm kids would play ball every evening after chores were done. Since I never went to high school, I didn't play organized ball until I got into the Navy in 1957. I was stationed in Pearl Harbor and played on both the ship's baseball team and fast pitch softball team. The softball season started in January and the baseball season started in April, so we could play on both teams. One year, our team went to Baltimore, Maryland to play in the All Navy Tournament. We also traveled all over the world playing softball. It was a great experience.

When I got out of the Navy in 1962, I kind of screwed up. Art Huinker talked his butt off trying to get me to go to Loras. I should've done it. Artie said, "Don't worry. We'll get you in." But I didn't do it. I started playing town ball with Dyersville then and played in 1962, 1963 and 1964. Then I went to play for my home town, Petersburg, and played until I was about 35 years old. I still filled in at Dyersville for some games during that time. Those three years at Dyersville were my best years because we had some great ball clubs. We went to the ABC nationals in '62 and '63. We should've won it in 1962. We had pitchers like Jim McAndrew, Eddie Watt, and Rich Folkers. All later pitched in the major leagues. Our home town pitcher, Sal Willenbring, was also very successful in the ABC. We used to tell him, "Sal, if you don't win this game, we're going to leave your---here and go home without you." If Sal would have had some good top notch coaching he could have gone a long way. He was big and strong and could really throw hard.

I also liked playing for Tom Jenk. If you were in a slump he would sit you down and let you think about what you might be doing

115

wrong. He and Dale Digman were two tough hitters in the lineup. If you needed a hit those two guys would usually come through. Of course, the best ballplayer I remember is Buzz Beatty. He was really something. He was fast, a good hitter and could hit with power. It seemed like he just had a knack for always being at the right place. I won't forget he once told me, "Jim to be a good base stealer, you have to get picked off once in awhile". He said this one time when we were playing in the ABC tournament. I led off with a hit and he batted second. We had signs with each other on whether the steal or hit-and-run was on. Anyway, I get picked off and he follows with a base hit. Then he gets picked off. He comes back to the bench and says, "See Jim, like I say, you have to get picked off now and then." I said, "You mean because you got picked off you're a good base stealer?"

The best pitcher I ever faced was Roger Fenwick who pitched in a lot of tournaments. He was from around Beloit, Wisconsin or in that area. He could throw hard and he nailed me a couple of times. After a while I was afraid to go up there again. A lefthander that gave me trouble was Rich Folkers from Waterloo. He struck me out five straight times one game. I faced Art Huinker a number of times and I couldn't hit him either.

One of my great memories was when I was in the eighth grade. I was the bat boy for Petersburg and they were invited to the Waterloo Courier Tournament in Waterloo. We took three greyhound buses out of Petersburg to travel there. The team was loaded, kind of an all-star team. Rocky Schiltz was playing first, Bob Krapfl played second, Buzz Beatty was playing short, Willie Moorman was in left and Dale Digman was in right. Eddie Schiltz was catching. We even had Joe Hoerner come in to relieve in the last inning and he struck out two guys to win the game. He was a senior in high school then. I was just 14 years old and I was warming him up before he went in. I couldn't hold him. But we got kicked out of the tournament because they said Hoerner was ineligible, for some reason. When we got back to Petersburg we even got the priest out of bed trying to figure out the documentation on why Hoerner was not eligible. As a young kid, you don't forget things like that.

Of course, some of my biggest thrills were watching our two sons play baseball, Tom and Chad. Chad played college ball at Mt. Mercy in Cedar Rapids and Tom pitched for six years in professional ball. Most of that time was with the Mets and he was one step away from going to the majors when he hurt his arm. He was traded to Baltimore his last year and then decided it was time to give it up and move on with his life.

Jims son Tom Wegmann
pitched at Middle Tenn.

Jims grandson Spencer Radabaugh
pitched at Loras Colleege.

LOCATION-LOCATION-LOCATION

Jack Wiland is a native of Bettendorf, Iowa. He graduated from the University of Iowa where he lettered two years in baseball. His entire career has been spent in education, teaching and coaching at the high school and junior college levels. He and his wife Pat reside in Palm Springs, California where Jack still teaches boys and girls golf at the local high school.

*A*fter graduating from Assumption High School in Davenport, I went to a junior college in California for two years and then transferred to the University of Iowa for the final two years, 1962-63.

Those two years playing baseball at Iowa were fun years. When I arrived, Coach Otto Vogel worked with me and changed my whole delivery. I wasn't getting enough drive off the rubber and I was throwing my curve ball three quarter arm instead of overhand. My whole performance improved with his help.

I was fortunate to pitch on a regular basis, both as a starter and reliever. Bob Gebhard and Jim McAndrew were on the staff and they threw a lot harder than I did. But I always had good control and ended up with a pretty good record. In my junior year, I won four games in relief and led the Big Ten with a .204 ERA. However, I didn't have enough innings to qualify for the conference ERA title. During my two years at Iowa I finished with an 11-2 record and a 2.62 ERA One of my highlights was beating Minnesota 3-2 in the 1962 opener against Minnesota who had an eleven game conference winning steak the previous year. The game was played in an hour and 25 minutes. After my senior year the White Sox talked to me about signing, but they only wanted to give me $500 bucks or something. I was married and starting a family and I told them "no".

I remember pitching against Wisconsin one day when Pat Richter and Rick Reichardt hit back to back home runs off me. Our centerfielder was Paul Krause, who later played football with the Vikings. He came in after the inning and said he didn't know how far those balls went because all he heard was "beep, beep" as they went over his head. Paul really could go get 'em; he saved me a lot with great catches.

After graduation I taught and coached in high school for four years, two at Dubuque Wahlert and two at Maquoketa Valley in Delhi, Iowa. During that time, in the mid sixties, I played semi-pro ball with several teams, including Monticello, Hopkinton, Balltown and several tournament games with Dyersville. My wife was working at K-Mart and some of the teams used to pay for the baby sitter. That was my pay. I still remember the strong interest in baseball in those small towns on Sunday afternoons and the tournament games during the week at night.

After moving back to California I continued to be involved with baseball for over 30 years. I taught and coached at Fallbrook High School there and also was also the pitching coach for the Fallbrook Junior College. I spent four summers with the Montreal Expos organization as a pitching instructor in the Pioneer League and the New York Penn League in Calgary, Canada. My teammate at Iowa, Bob Gebhard, was the Expos' minor league director and he helped me get that assignment. During that time, I became good friends with Duke Snider, the former Dodger Hall of Famer who was associated with the Expos at that time. I attended his funeral last year. All of the living former Dodgers were there.

I retired in 2005 but still coach the boys and girls golf team here at Desert Hot Springs High School.

"Greg Maddux could put a baseball through a life saver if you asked him."

Joe Morgan

LOVE TO PLAY

Dale Klein, one of six brothers, is a native of Balltown, Iowa. He played semi-pro baseball for Balltown and the Waterloo Merchants in the 1980's. The following article appeared in the Dubuque Telegraph Herald following major leagues' aversion of a strike in 2002.

I realize MLB averted another strike, but I couldn't have cared less if it did strike. They cut it too close and again have taken it too far.

One reason I would not have missed it is because I get my baseball fix via the Telegraph Herald Web site sports section. There is nothing like the baseball that is played back in eastern Iowa. Whether it be semi-pro, college or high school baseball, it's played in its purest form.

These people play the game because they love to play the game. It's that simple.

These are people you work with and can relate to as our parents could with the baseball players of the past.

To relate to today's player, average salary of $2.4 million, we would have to be lucky enough to win the lottery and when cashing in the ticket, utter, "It's not about the money."

I remember growing up, with the Balltown baseball field in my back yard. Thinking back, I can't remember a day we didn't play ball. We didn't call each other to get a game together, we just naturally all went to the field knowing that others would be there to play. When it rained, we would take the game to our basement and use anything we could that wouldn't break the windows, with the exception of one time. The ball might be a sock, a newspaper wrapped with tape, or that softball-shaped thing that mom used to scrub the baked-on food in the bottom of pans before there were no-stick surfaces. The bat could be a stick, broom handle, pool cue or our hands if nothing else was available. One way or another, we were going to play baseball or something that resembled it based on what we had and where we were.

There is nothing like the semi-pro league in eastern Iowa around the Dubuque area. After playing for Balltown, I played several years in a semi-pro league for the Waterloo Merchants while attending the University of Northern Iowa. Don't get me wrong, it was very competitive, but not every little town had a team like they do near Dubuque.

I just want to thank the TH for putting all the semi-pro scores on the Web site because it is still very fun to follow from a distance. Seeing the names I used to play against and the new names from the high schools and colleges finding a roster spot to play when their season ends is what it's all about.

About 10 years ago, I moved out of Iowa to Colorado. I wasn't able to find a similar league out here either, and after several years, softball didn't seem to provide enough of a challenge. So I traded my spikes for hiking boots, as did my younger brother Jeff ("Coop") now living in San Dimas, California. It's not baseball, but hiking to the top of a 14,000 foot peak (I've completed 11 of Colorado's 54) has its challenges and can be equally satisfying as winning the Dyersville tournament (I was on the 1983 Balltown team that beat the Dubuque Merchants, 12-9, for the championship).

On a recent trip this summer, Jeff and I hiked to the summit of Colorado's highest peak, Mount Elbert. At 14,400 feet, Mount Elbert also is the second-highest peak in the lower 48 states. The hike was 7.6 miles round trip, with 4,000 feet of elevation gain (very steep). We made it up to the summit in about four hours. We refueled our bodies with Cliff bars and Gatorade, took in the incredible views and rested a bit.

Then I looked at my brother and in my best Kevin Costner voice said, "Hey you wanna have a catch."

He replied, "Of course."

With that we opened our backpacks, pulled out our gloves and had a catch at 14,400 feet. We received a few crazy looks, but most of the people nodded in approval as if to be swept back to their childhood playing days – wishing they had brought their gloves to the summit, too.

Baseball is something that will always be with me no matter where I am because of the love I had for playing the game growing up – not because of any MLB player of the past, present or uncertain future.

The reason we played catch on the summit was to thank the fans that followed and supported us, the coaches that coached us, the people we competed against, the teammates we played with, Mom and Dad, who made it all possible, and to remember the incredible amount of fun we had playing the game.

If you're from eastern Iowa, don't ever worry about losing MLB to a strike, just focus on the wonderful, competitive game of semi-pro baseball you will always have, played by the people you really know.

When's the next old-timers game?

Dale was recently asked about that article and if he has the same view today.

"Today, I feel stronger than ever about the words I wrote back in 2002."

He said this feeling was strongly reinforced when he played in an Old Timers game at Rickardsville in August 2008. The game was really a fundraiser for his brother, Gary and his family who were hit by a destructive flood in Cedar Rapids three months earlier. The fact that his skills had obviously decreased was beside the point. "The small communities of Eastern Iowa rose to the occasion for someone in need and they used baseball, the game they love to do it."

That memorable day reminded Dale of the time the family closed their dad's (Ferdie) funeral in 2004, just a few months after they all shared a Klein family, baseball-awesome day at the Field of Dreams movie site. They repeated Terrance Mann's <u>Field of Dreams</u> quote, "These stories and memories remind us of all that once was good and when we all meet in heaven, will be good again."

BASEBALL AND MOTHERHOOD

Joanie Klein lives in Balltown, Iowa where she has resided for over 50 years. She and her husband, Ray, "Ferdie" raised six boys: Steve, Joe, Gary, Dale, Jeff, and Ron, all of whom played baseball at various levels. Five of them played semi-pro baseball for the Balltown team. During one semi-pro game, four of them were all in the game at the same time.

*O*ur home in Balltown backed right up to the town baseball diamond. So the boys were always playing there with other town kids when the weather was nice. In bad weather they played in our large garage on the lower level. But they knew that when they came home they had to do yard work and help their dad, who always had a huge garden, before they would eat.

They were good boys, but they still were boys. I never knew what I would see when I came home. One time I walked into the living room and noticed an out of place shadow. I thought a light bulb had burned out. What happened was they had been playing catch/ baseball in the living room with a rolled up sock and the sock got stuck up in the light fixture on the ceiling. Another time Gary, Dale and Jeff were playing ball in the rock quarry behind the ball field— why I'll never know. Anyway Jeff fell on a sharp rock and really started bleeding. They came home through the basement garage and tried to clean him up before coming upstairs so I would not know about it. But by the time they got upstairs, the white handkerchief put on the cut to stop the bleeding was completely red, so we had to take him to the doctor for stitches.

With six boys playing there was always a game going on somewhere - PeeWee, Little League, Babe Ruth, Junior Legion, high school, or semi-pro town team. Ferdie and I went to all the games whenever we could. Sometimes we had to split up because often there were games at different places on the same day. It seems like I was always washing uniforms, mending them or putting on patches,

125

but that was ok. I didn't mind because I knew that it was important to them.

I enjoyed watching them play, but I was always afraid of injuries. One time Joe and Gary injured their ankles in the same inning, in the same game, on the same base. Joe injured his ankle sliding into third base, Gary pinch-ran for him and injured his ankle on the very next play on a pick-off play. Both came home on crutches.

All in all, I am so thankful that baseball played such an important role in their lives, because it kept them from doing other things that could have gotten them in trouble. It was so important to them that we did not go on very many summer vacations—baseball always came first. They never wanted to miss a game and showed up for every game.

Our last family outing before Ferdie died was to *The Field of Dreams* in August 2003. Dale came home from Colorado and arranged the trip for the whole family. We still have a picture of that day in front of the white picket fence and *The Field of Dreams* house.

"All that I am, or hope to be, I owe to my angel mother."
                                                    Abraham Lincoln

A KEY "LINK" IN BALLTOWN
BASEBALL OPERATIONS
By Jim Brimeyer

Lyle Link was a Balltown native who grew up on a nearby farm. He faithfully served as scorekeeper and statistician for Balltown for two decades.

Any baseball team depends on all of its members to function. That includes players, managers, coaches, bat boys, and statisticians. Small town baseball in Balltown was no different. For many years, Lyle Link served as scorekeeper for the town's semi-pro team, most notably under managers Earl Rettenmaier and Leon Cummer. Lyle never missed a game, whether a Sunday league contest or semi-pro tournament games. He faithfully sat on the bench and supported the Balltown players with his scorebook and positive, caring attitude.

Lyle never was named MVP in a tournament or ever received much credit, much less reimbursement for his services. Yet he was the epitome of what small town Iowa baseball is all about - giving for the good of others and the team. Lyle served in the United States Air Force where he was stationed in California for four years. Following his discharge in 1954, he assumed the duties of scorekeeper and continued uninterrupted into the early seventies.

At most games that Lyle kept score, his entire family - wife Elaine, daughters Pat and Peg, and son Kevin - accompanied him, whether Sundays or week nights, whether home or away. Lyle's wife Elaine recalls, "I worked at Osco Drug for years, and when I got off work, I would hurry home because Lyle would have the car packed with the kids inside and ready to go to the games." They rarely missed a Balltown game.

Lyle would faithfully take his spot on the bench and record every pitch, every hit, every out, every inning. He would inform the Balltown players of their batting order each inning and inform the defense of the opponent's upcoming hitters to help their positioning. And he always had that patented smile on his face. He would encourage the players when they made mistakes and celebrate and praise their successes. After the game, Lyle's work was not finished. He would take his scorebook home and calculate team batting averages and pitching records in his spare time. Manager Earl Rettenmaier stated, "Lyle Link was very conscientious about his job as scorekeeper. He kept such accurate pitch counts that I even relied on him to let me know when a pitcher was reaching his maximum pitch count."

During home games, Lyle was also in charge of monitoring the return of foul balls that were hit behind the backstop into the parking lot or over the hill. He would arrange for youngsters to chase the foul balls and return them to the Balltown bench, where he had a stash of dimes from which he awarded each ball retriever ten cents per ball returned. On a good afternoon, a youngster could leave the game with a profitable fifty cents in his pocket, a hefty amount in those days for a fun day at the ball field.

Lyle Link never received praise or acclaim for his work. He wasn't famous or a big name player, but every Balltown player and opponent recognized his smiling face. Like all small town baseball participants, he simply gave of himself because he loved the game and it was the thing to do to help make things work.

What did Babe Ruth, Rogers Hornsby, Ted Williams, and Willie Mays do in their first major league at bat?

All of them struck out!

BEST SEAT IN THE PARK

Al Denlinger is a native of Zwingle, Iowa. He worked for the Dubuque Packing Company for 34 years. He moved to Maquoketa in 1968 where he helped revive the team that had been inactive for a number of years. Al is a member of the Dubuque County Hall of Fame. He and his wife, Marilyn, presently reside in Dubuque, Iowa.

*M*y semi-pro career started right after graduating from high school at the age of sixteen in 1947. In those days, that's about all you had to do around those small towns is play baseball. The regular catcher, Bob Huber, broke his leg and they told me, "Get in there and catch." I said, "Oh, ok." I was scared to death, but after I started catching that became my regular position and I loved it. I caught for about 25 years, into my forties.

Then I moved to Maquoketa and helped them start up a team again since the Maquoketa Bears had been gone for a number of years. We called ourselves the Indians and ended up with a pretty good team. I managed the team for about ten years and also played occasionally, like pinch hitting and filling in when we were short of players. We won the Prairie League about four years in a row and also finished runners up in the state ABC Tournament at Watkins a couple of teams. A team from Des Moines beat us out. Dick Wold and Haven Schmidt played for us. Of course Haven had played professional ball at a high level for a number of years. And Dick played with us for a long time. He was quite a ballplayer. He really loved the game.

One of the best recollections I have was when we played at Zwingle. We would go up to get the diamond ready, and those darn cows would be lying down on the diamond. Before taking batting practice we had to chase them off the field, and when they got up they would crap all over the field. We would use scoop shovels to clean off the diamond before we could start. Now they have a real nice field there called Loras Collins Field.

Playing at Pleasant Grove was also quite an experience. They had a creek behind left field and long fly balls would go into that creek. In back of home plate, there was a big screen that hung over the backstop to keep foul balls from flying across the road. So you were sort of caged in back there. The first time I caught there a foul ball went up and came right down and hit me on top of the head.

There are many good memories playing at Zwingle. One day we were playing and Don Wagner was pitching for the other team. He had a real loose fitting uniform. I hit a ball back to him and it went up his sleeve into his shirt. He was flailing around the mound trying to get it out. The runner on second scored and I ended up on second base with an infield double.

Of course, Winky Hoerner was always around Zwingle. In fact, he was my first cousin. He was quite a Winky and loved the game. He ran the tavern there for awhile. Before a tournament game at Dyersville or some other place, he would go to the gas station, fill up his car and take off. When he got back he had a pitcher or some other players lined up. One year they won the Dyersville Tournament with only one player from Zwingle, Lucky John Laughlin.

Hiring pitchers for tournaments was really a big deal in those days. The best pitcher I ever saw was my brother-in-law, Darrold Satchell, who pitched as high as Triple A. But he didn't pitch much around here. He and Haven Schmidt signed together. As far as the best pitchers I faced, there were a number of them that gave me trouble. I would have to say Artie Huinker was the best left handed pitcher and Tom Brietbach was the best right handed pitcher. Artie had a great curve ball. I remember one time he threw me a shoulder high pitch and I thought I'm really going to kill this baby and the catcher scooped it out of the dirt. Dick Wold told me that when Dyersville went to the ABC Tournament in Battle Creek, there were some scouts talking to him about coming back into pro ball But he had a teaching career then and wasn't interested. Breitbach had all the pitches, had great control and was a very nice guy along with it.

Over the years I was always called "Toad". My brother gave me that name when I was very young. He said, "You're Toad. That's what we're going to call you, Toad." So that's how I became known as "Toad".

Playing and managing all those years are memories that will always stay with me.

Editor's Note: When I asked Al about interesting stories, I first told him of the story Dick Wold told about him (Al) in Chapter 6. Before I got very far into the scenario, Al laughed and said, "I know what you're talking about." Al verified the story. I asked if he was ok to put that story in the book and he said, "Sure." A true stand up guy!

Tim McCarver is the only catcher to lead the league in triples. He hit 13 in 1966, edging out teammate Lou Brock who had 12.

SPECIAL DELIVERY

Frank Dardis is a native of Peosta, Iowa, While on active duty with the U.S. Air Force, he received a Presidential Appointment to the Air Force Academy. He subsequently dropped out of the Academy to get married and transferred to Loras College where he graduated with a degree in Accounting and lettered four years in baseball. He is the local postmaster for the U.S. Postal Service in Peosta. Frank, his wife Mary Beth, and family reside in Peosta.

*P*eosta has a rich tradition in semi-pro baseball. I started playing with the town team as a sophomore year in high school around 1969 and still have not officially quit. I played with and against a lot of players who were more talented than me, but I was blessed with a good body that has held up. I manage to get in some games now and then with the local team, and still play age-bracket baseball in the over 50-55 league in Florida and Arizona for a number of years. Paul Scherrman from Farley and I have played quite a bit together down there. I enjoy the heck out of playing with him. Most of my career has been as a pitcher but I have also played first base. I managed for about 25 years but gave that up in 2005 and started umpiring. I umpire between 100 and 150 games a year - high school, semi pro, and a few college games. It's a way for me to stay with the game that I love.

We have some real nice ball parks in the area now, major league style like Peosta and Farley. But two of my favorite diamonds are still Pleasant Grove and Balltown. Pleasant Grove has the cow pasture and at Balltown, they still pick rocks out of the infield and have the tavern nearby. To me, those places represent what Dubuque County Baseball is all about.

A favorite story of mine occurred when I was umpiring about ten years ago in the Holy Cross Tournament. My partner that day was a local guy, Matt Schuster, who brought his 11 year old son along. While the teams were warming up it was discovered that one team only had seven players. So rather than forfeit the game, we came up with the idea that Matt's son would play and Matt, himself, would also play while they were in the field, and then umpire the bases when his team was at bat. Of course, the Holy Cross Athletic Committee gave their approval because they wanted the game to be played so the fans would stick around and drink a few more beverages. I came up with the idea that if Matt gave me any grief when he came to bat that I would throw him out of the game. It would be the first time in Dubuque County baseball that one umpire threw the other out of the game. Of course, we were only joking and did not have to follow through with my idea.

Another time when I was managing we were playing in the Kieler Tournament. One of our players, Kevin Beck, was a good ball player and he was squawking at the plate umpire's strike zone. Later in the game, Kevin was batting and I was on deck batting behind him. I heard the umpire start heckling Kevin. I called time and I said to the umpire that I apologize for Kevin disagreeing with his balls and strikes, but he could not heckle my batter. The umpire said, "Yes I can because I'm the head umpire." I told him I would have to report him to the Umpires Association. He just laughed and said: "No you can't you goof ball, because there is no association. We're contracted by the home team." He was right, there was no association at that time and that's the way it is today.

Another funny story occurred in the Worthington Tournament in the 1980's. Dennis Rima, a great guy, would always cross himself when he came to the plate. Two guys on our bench, Jim Callahan and Kevin Beck, were talking to each other about this being a little over the top. The first time up Dennis hits one over the center field fence and everybody is congratulating him. Of course, the next time up he crossed himself again. Jim and Kevin are sitting together yet and Jim just kind of rolls his eyes. Dennis hit another home run. He comes to the plate the third time and crosses himself again. Kevin is just laughing because Kevin is rolling his eyes again. Dennis hits his third home run in a row. Jim turns to Kevin and said, "Maybe I'll start crossing myself when I'm at the plate." Dennis comes up the fourth time that night and hit a deep fly that the centerfielder caught right in front of the fence. Jim looks at Kevin and says, "Well I guess I'm back to not crossing myself." True story.

My best memories involved the *Field of Dreams* movie. I was lucky enough to be picked as one of the Ghost Players. As a result, we got to travel around the world and play teams in other countries. I got to take my wife on some of those trips which we could not have afforded on our own. Those trips were really fun. One time my teammates set me up with the Japanese umpires. I had the reputation of having a good pick-off move to first base and my opponents always accused me of balking. So they told the umpires to call a balk on me. The Japanese umpires all came to the mound and said, "You're balking. You're balking." My teammates were just rolling in the dugout because they got their revenge.

I just hope that fifty years from now we'll still be able to talk about semi-pro baseball in this area. We have a good tradition in this area and I would like to see it continue.

> *"If you dwell on statistics, you get shortsighted. If you aim for consistency, the numbers will be there at the end."*
> Tom Seaver

MEMORIES OF
TOWN TEAM BASEBALL

*Jack Marlowe is a lifelong resident of Ma-
quoketa, Iowa. He started his journalis-
tic career as a part time sports writer with
the Maquoketa Sentinel Press in 1962. He
eventually became a fulltime sports editor
that included a stay with the Bellevue Herald Leader. Now retired, Jack still writes a
monthly sports column, Sports Slants, for
the Maquoketa Sentinel Press.*

*D*ad played baseball in the 1920s on a neighborhood team
in Fairfield Township when he was courting Mom. They played
in pastures against similar teams like Pea Ridge, Stony Point and
Buckeye. I became hooked on baseball before television and before
I even realized games were on the radio. We played softball during
recess at a one-room country school using our own rules. I had a
dime store glove and played with tacked bats and balls covered with
tape. There weren't any organized youth leagues. When World
War II ended I was ten years old. I remember watching the Maquoketa Bears who developed a strong team. Players dug the post holes
when lights were installed in 1948. The first game under the lights
was against the Prairie League All-Stars before a crowd of 1500.
With the lights, the team could schedule 40 games a season.

My background as a player was limited to a brief and humble
high school and junior legion career, a couple of seasons with the
Maquoketa Bears, and a short term of helping with the organization
of local teams. Despite my unimpressive playing career, I became
a baseball fanatic. For years I collected everything I could that was
associated with baseball – baseball cards, books, magazines, even
equipment. I have sold a lot of stuff, but am still stupid enough
to continue buying different things. I have over 1,000 hard cover
books on baseball. I never married, so I'm just happy to be by myself, surrounded by all my collection of sports, especially baseball.

Even though my baseball experiences are primarily centered on the Maquoketa and surrounding area, I also had the opportunity to watch a fair number of games in the Dubuqueland area and see some of the great players in that area. Fan support of teams in the 1950's are just memories. Attending games was the thing to do and fans worshipped their hometown players. Bleachers were filled and cars lined foul lines risking windshields to foul balls and bad throws.

Some of my highlight memories:

Loras Simon played for Pleasant Grove as a sixteen year old and stayed active in baseball for over 40 years. He was coaching third base one evening for Bernard when fans discussed his age. A fan said Simon was 56 years old and had played nine innings the previous Sunday.

In June 1991 Larry Stolte was asked to play nine innings in right field for Louden, managed by his son, Stacy. It marked the sixth decade for Stolte to play for Lowden. He started in 1948 and spent 30 seasons as their manager.

Marvin Ruggeberg, an Elwood farmer, started his baseball career as a left-handed pitcher. He played until he was 37, then managed the team before switching to umpiring. He still was umpiring at the age of 79. Marvin worked 152 baseball and softball games in one summer.

Tom Breitbach from Dubuque was one of the craftiest pitchers in the area. He always was in top shape and was as close to Greg Maddux in pitching style as there was in the Dubuque area. Many hitters returned to the bench shaking their heads after facing him.

John Moran, who later became a Catholic priest, was an outstanding catcher and power hitter from the Cascade area.

Loras Collins and Zwingle are synonymous. He insists that he was more of a thrower than a pitcher, but during one game no Andrew batter hit the ball out of the infield. Zwingle's field today is named Loras Collins Field.

Larry Lambe, a Zwingle outfielder, received the hustler award one year in the Cascade Tournament. He played without a left arm that had been amputated due to a farm accident. Lambe had little trouble catching and throwing the ball, and was a good contact hitter.

While in high school, Cliff Dirks of Wyoming overcame misfortune of having thrown balls that killed two players within eight months. One occurred when he hit a batter and the other was the result of a pickoff play. He was a true gentleman and remained an active player and manager in his hometown.

Perhaps the longest game in Maquoketa history went 16 innings and ended in a 15-15 tie in 1959 in Wyoming. It was called at 1:00 a.m. DST.

Gerald Koch pitched eight innings in relief and was the winning pitcher when the Maquoketa Bears defeated the Dubuque Merchants, 12-10 in 12 innings in 1953. He had pitched a nine inning complete game for Preston in the afternoon.

Cousins Glen and Harold "Bud" Myatt made hay together in the afternoon in 1948. That night they were opposing pitchers in a game between Maquoketa and Lost Nation, won by Glen's Lost Nation Team 1-0.

Dick Wold was one of the most respected hitters in the area. In 1970, the left-handed hitting Wold batted .523 for the Maquoketa Indians. He went through the entire season without striking out.

Pat Weber, in his 40's is still pitching strong for the Cascade Reds. He has notched over 300 wins in his semi-pro career.

Today, Lenny Tekippe at Rickardsville and Paul Scherrman at Farley rank among the long term managers in the Prairie League.

Editor's Note: Jack's recent article in the Maquoketa Sentinel-Press on Maqouketa baseball appears in the EXTRA INNINGS chapter.

PUT ME IN COACH...

I'M READY TO

PLAY......TODAY!

The following individuals followed through with interviews or provided information in response to ads in the local papers, inviting all interested parties to contact the author.

Victor Sprengelmeyer – East Dubuque, IL

My father was Lucian Edward Sprengelmeyer, a native Dubuquer, whose name gave the reporters of his day fits for spelling. He was sometimes called "String" by his teammates because of his tall and lanky build. Dad's younger brother was Walter who also played professional and semi-pro baseball with a number of teams, starring for a few seasons in the old Western League. Sometimes the brothers formed a battery, and sometimes they opposed one another. Both had strong arms from thousands of hours of playing catch with each other since boyhood.

When they played in the 1930's, there were two leagues, the Dubuque Municipal League and the Maquoketa Valley League. Dad pitched for the Dubuque Koolmotors team in the Municipal League and they had a dominant team. There was a big rivalry between the Koolmotors team managed by Gerald "Red" McAleece and the Dan Patch team managed by Red's brother.

One of Dad's closest friends was teammate Everett "Shorty" Aikens. From what Dad told me and photos I have seen, Shorty and Dad were exact opposites in build. Shorty was a steeplejack by trade, an acrobat, daredevil, stuntman and all around showman. Between games of a hot July 4th doubleheader in Ryan, Shorty talked to the acrobatic pilot of a bi-plane. The next thing people saw was Shorty wing-walking during the bi-plane show. He later told his teammates he thought it would be a good way to cool off between games.

141

Dad also told me about a special promotion in Wrigley Field one day in the 30's. It was a doubleheader between two semi-pro teams in one game and then the Cubs played a regular game in the other. The Dubuque All Star team, heavily staffed with Koolmotors players, played another Midwest All-Star team. With Dad pitching, it was a scoreless game in the bottom of the 9th. Midwest All-Stars had two outs with a runner on second. On a 3-2 count the batter hit a fly ball to left field which the left fielder misplayed and the winning run scored. The left fielder's name was "Boom" Mueller, one of the Koolmotors' regulars and a lifetime friend of Dad. Mueller was the last survivor of the Koolmotors' team. I had occasion to visit with him several time in his last years. He was still apologizing for his error in Wrigley Field 60 years after the fact. Dad was given a military style ribbon for his participation in that game, and it remained one of his treasured possessions all his life. Today, my son has that prized possession in memory of his grandfather.

In his later years Dad would watch the major league games on television and scoff at the performances. He said that any pitcher who could not throw strikes or pitch a full nine innings was grossly overpaid and would be lucky to be selected in the old Municipal League.

Lucian Sprengelmeyer was inducted into the Dubuque County Baseball Hall of Fame in 1988, the second year of the Hall's existence.

Eldon "Junior" Pickel - Kieler, Wisconsin

The Kieler ball diamond was set in a hole. The outfield had a steep bank from left field to right center. All outfielders had to learn to go uphill on fly balls and adjust to the flight as they were going up the bank. The Lange brothers were interesting fans who would sit in their chairs on the hill and yell when the home team came to bat, "Hit it in the cornfield." There was usually corn planted in back of the outfield fence, and any homerun over the fence landed in the corn. As a youth watching home games, these family names would usually pop up all the time: Richards, Burlage, Jansen, Kunkel, Droessler, Pickel, Kaiser and Leibfried.

Early in the 70's when my age group started to play, we would fund our operations by selling squares on a poster to local merchants. Our manager for a long time was Gary Leibfried who was a great leader. If people only knew everything Gary did to keep baseball alive in Kieler, they would appreciate him more. Jerry Jansen was one of the best players I remember watching. He was a great fielder and hitter. Kieler competed in two leagues, the Prairie League and the Tri-States League. The tri-states league consisted of Shullsburg, Benton, Belmont, Platteville, East Dubuque, Galena and Hazel Green The winner of the league would be invited to the state tourney in Madison. Kieler made many trips there and finished runner up one year.

James Whitfield - Volga, Iowa

My father told me this story that he remembered from the early 1930's. Volga had a real good team and a real good pitcher. They played Independence at the fair in Strawberry Point. There was a lot of betting going on. After the bets were all down, Independence took the field and they had a black battery from the Negro Leagues. Rube Foster was the pitcher and Bill Booker was the catcher. Volga got beat pretty good. After one of the Volga batters came back to the bench after striking out, my father heard my grandfather Henry ask the guy, "Well how big was the ball?" The guy answered: "About the size of a small pea, Henry." What happened was no one from Volga knew that Independence had imported this Negro battery because they had warmed up out of sight before the game. A Volga fan and a guy from Fayette made a bet before the game and they had been good friends a long time. One accused the other that he knew what was going on before they bet. Of course, the other guy denied it. They never spoke together again.

In the late 1940's, the Elkader Vets had a good team. Jack Dittmer and Glen Drahn from the University of Iowa played for them. They also had Ken Keister from Monona, Bill Stout from Upper Iowa and Moose Faber, nephew of former Hall of Fame pitcher, Red Faber. One time Humboldt played there and they were managed by the Brooklyn Dodger catcher, Mickey Owen. The former National League umpire, George Magerkurth, umped behind the plate. He really barked out the balls and strikes and that was a big hit with everybody. Of course, they rehashed the famous dropped third strike by Mickey Owen when Tommy Henrich was batting in the 1941 World Series.

143

The Vets also played different traveling teams during those good years. Max Lanier's All-Stars had players like Lanier, Sal Maglie, Lou Klein and other major leaguers. The Indianapolis Clowns also came through and Henry Aaron played for them. He was only 16 years old at the time. I saw the game but never realized what a star he would become. Those games would draw over 2,000 people.

I played semi-pro baseball until the age of 25 when I had to quit because of farming. Besides Volga, I played for West Union, Elkader, as well as Colesberg and Guttenberg in the Dyersville Tournament. I also played one year at Upper Iowa. I almost hit a triple down the right field line against the famed Lefty Meyers, but the ball was just foul. That's the closest I ever got to a hit against him. I also batted against Tommy Breitbach from Dubuque and Art Huinker from Festina. I didn't do any good against them either.

Dennis Rima - Dubuque

I played for the Peosta Cubs in the Prairie League in the late 80's and 90's. I was involved in the "Play of the Tournament" in the championship game of the Cascade Tournament one year. My brother David was pitching, my brother Neil was at shortstop and I was playing second. The opposing team had runners on first and second with one out. The batter hit a line drive which ricocheted off my brother Dave's back and went directly in the air to Neil playing shortstop, and he relayed it to me at second base for a double play. The runner on second thought the ball was going through after he saw it hit my brother and was heading toward third. So the "Play of the Tournament" was "Rima to Rima to Rima".

Robert Brimeyer - Dubuque

The general location of what has been the ball diamond in Balltown for many years used to be an oats field farmed by Leon Breitbach. In 1936, after the oats was cut, the ballplayers moved the bundles of oats and stacked them along the fence, and made a ball field. Those players included Ralph Klein, Joe Strumburger, Eldon Pfohl, Cletus and Billy Link, Arnold and Clarence Gansemer. Cletus Link was the manager. He was a POW in World War II. He returned as manager for a couple of years after the war, until Harold Beatty moved to Balltown and took over. The diamond was re-graded in 1951 and is still used today. I remember there were always a lot of arguments in those early days because they always
144

used local umpires and that caused many problems. However, Balltown and Cassville, Wisconsin always got along and would drink beer together after the game.

Dennis Smeltzer - Waterloo, Iowa

I grew up in Lowden, Iowa where we had a town team for many years. Larry Stolte managed the team from 1955 to 1998. We played in the Corn Belt League, composed of teams along Highway 30. When that league died, they played teams around the Dubuque area. Thursday night was town team baseball night where the stores stayed open until a half hour before the game and it was the place to be. Beer was drunk, hot dogs and maid rites sold, and bets on the game were made. Foul balls got you a dime and if you picked up a case of pop bottles you would get a bottle free.

Leon Sigwarth - Balltown, Iowa

Developing a passion for baseball and competing with the best of the Dubuque area players has given me a gift of confidence that carried with me all my life.

I have many fond memories of the years I played for Balltown. One of them occurred in Holy Cross when the announcer called for a pause to look at a unique situation. Three brothers—Leon, Joe, and Bill Sigwarth were on base and the fourth brother, Herb, was batting.

Another time, after playing in many tournament games in a week, my mother figured out if you win, you get to play again. She followed me out the door before the next game and said in her broken Luxemberger scolding voice, "You're going out too many nights, I pray that you lose." Such things you don't forget.

Brian Schueller - Waukee, Iowa

Growing up near Sherrill, Iowa, a town of just over 200, a small community was drawn together by baseball. No other sport was able to do that during the decade of the 1980's. Teammates and fans attended school and church together. If you went to the ballpark, you were bound to know almost everyone there.

This led to rivalries specifically with Balltown, Rickardsville, and Holy Cross. Relatives living in these other communities and marriages between families across these communities led to good-natured ribbing. Queen pageants associated with local tournaments allowed siblings of the players to compete against each other. Small parades were held at times with some of the local tournaments, allowing those not associated directly with the baseball team to take part in the community as well.

Today, I live in Waukee, Iowa, a western suburb of Des Moines. Des Moines alone has over 200,000 people with about 570,000 in the five county metro area. Growing up in Sherrill with a population of just 200, I was able to play baseball pretty much whenever I wanted. Today, the city of Des Moines, and surrounding metro area, has ZERO public baseball fields. In order for our local league to have sustained success, we have to rent local high school and college fields in order to play games. The opportunities to secure additional dates on those fields to hold a practice are few and far between.

To say I miss small-town baseball and the atmosphere that surrounded it would be a huge understatement.

Dave Bowersock - Tucson, Arizona

I played high school and legion ball in Newton, Kansas before playing six years of semi-pro ball in that area. Then I attended the University of Wichita, now Wichita State, and played four years there. During one of those summers I played in the Amateur Baseball League of America, a league that was sponsored by major league teams. It was a chance for the big league clubs to evaluate talent while they could still keep their amateur status. I belonged to the Boston Braves organization. After the first summer the manager told me the higher ups wanted me to come back the next season, but he told me, "Son, you're a good ball player but you'll never make it

146

to the majors so I would advise you to go back to college, get an education and start a family." I was disappointed at the time but he was ABSOLUTELY RIGHT. My semi-pro years playing for Newton and Peabody, Kansas included three appearances in the prestigious NBC Tournament in Wichita. They were baseball crazy in that area in those days. They would even hire players whenever they could. In fact, one of the Wichita teams was composed almost entirely of former major league players. After college I joined the Air Force, went through pilot training and eventually became a Commander of a B-47 bomber crew.

A funny story occurred that one year when I was playing in the Amateur League. We were playing in Abilene, Kansas and I knew the opposing pitcher pretty well. I came to bat and, just for fun, I pointed out to left field, kind of like Babe Ruth did in the World Series against the Cubs. Be darned if I didn't hit a homerun almost to the spot I was pointing. My parents had driven a long distance to see the game. My dad was so proud he told me how good I was and how far I was going to go. At the end of the summer, my manager told me I wasn't good enough to make the majors so that was the end of that. I guess he thought I would never be another Babe Ruth.

Stan Wagner - Sun Prairie, Wisconsin

Baseball was a big part of my life for a number of years. After high school, I attended Loras College for one year and then transferred to the University of Wisconsin. Loras had two good pitchers my freshman year so I did not pitch very much. I lost a year of eligibility by transferring but I was in the regular rotation at Wisconsin my junior and senior years.

In the summer of 1961, I pitched one game for Guttenberg against Dyersville in the Dyersville Tournament. They even offered to fly me down, but my dad and I drove from Sun Prairie. Anyway we beat Dyersville and that was a big deal. I remember in the last inning, Dyersville had the tying run in scoring position with two outs and Jack Dittmer at the plate. The manager, Herb Borcherding, came to the mound and asked if I wanted pitch to Dittmer or walk him and pitch to the cleanup hitter who had hit a home run earlier in the game. I elected to walk Dittmer, a former major leaguer, and pitch to the cleanup hitter. I struck him out to end the game.

My biggest claim to fame was pitching for Wisconsin my senior year, 1962. We played Michigan in a Saturday doubleheader. Michigan was leading the Big Ten at the time. I won the first game and we were trailing by a run in the last inning of the second game. The coach asked if I could pitch an inning. So I said, "Sure." My folks left after the first game and took my glove with them, so I had to borrow a glove. They didn't score in the top half, and in the bottom half we had two outs and our third baseman hit a triple. Pat Richter, who later became Athletic Director, was up. They changed pitchers and brought in their ace who had pitched the day before. On the first pitch Richter hit a home run and we won the game, so I was credited with two wins in a four hour period. Michigan went on to win the NCAA championship in the College World Series at Omaha, Nebraska.

I played over ten years of semi-pro in the Madison area. In 1966, a Milwaukee team won the state NBC tournament and picked me up when they went to the nationals in Wichita, Kansas. We ended up in the final four. I still remember the final game we lost. In extra innings we had the bases loaded and nobody out and tried the suicide squeeze which resulted in a double play and we ended up losing.

Duane Hagan - Millville, Iowa

I grew up on a farm in the Garber area of northeast Iowa. As a youngster I would throw rocks and every once in awhile was able to pick off a bird sitting on the high line wires. I played over 22 years of semi-pro baseball around Guttenberg, Dyersville and West Union. My baseball highlight was relieving Whitey Ford while we were both stationed at the Fort Monmouth army base in New Jersey in 1951. I don't remember the specific circumstances but I did retire the side without a run after relieving him. Two semi-pro games I will always remember occurred in the Cascade and Dyersville tournaments. In 1957 I pitched a 1-0 game against Key West. They had a strong team that included the Hoerner brothers and they were undefeated in 19 games. The funny thing is I didn't feel that I had that much stuff that night. It was just one of those nights where ev-

148

erything worked.   Then one night against Independence in the Dyersville Tournament in that same era, I couldn't get anybody out in
the first inning and they scored ten runs. They had a good left hander
by the name of Rocky Rothrock and beat us 10-0.   So those were
two games that I will never forget, for different reasons, of course.

Bob Meyer - Dubuque, Iowa (Another Bob Meyer)

Growing up in Key West in the 50's and 60's meant that you
were exposed to a lot of baseball.   They had two teams when I was
in my early teens, the Key West Ramblers A team and the Key West
Ramblers B team.   We youngsters would call them the "Big Guys"
because they were all in their late teens, 20's and 30's.   We would
get their wooden bats that were cracked and tape them for our pick
up games.   We would also go to their ball field the next day and

try to find lost balls beyond the outfield
for our use.   We would lie on the ground
and roll through the weeds until we felt a
lump and that was usually a lost baseball.
We never had to buy any balls that way.

There was a local store owner in Key
West, Ray Hanten, who had some prop-
erty behind his store.   He spent his own money and had the property
leveled for a ball diamond for us local kids.   We called ourselves the
Ramblers "C" team.   We never played anyone except ourselves

I also remember yelling at the umpires when we went to the Big
Guys' games.   We yelled things like: "GET NEW GLASSES!" and
"OPEN YOUR EYES!" and "ARE YOU BLIND?"   We weren't
very nice.   Years later I helped coach little league in Arizona and I
would jump all over the kids for doing the same thing.   Actually the
parents were worse but I couldn't control them.

LaVern Pape – Dubuque, Iowa

Some of my earliest memories go back to the early 30's when
I was just seven or eight years old.   My dad took me to a ballgame
at Balltown where there was a farm field behind the church sheds.
The bases were sand or dirt bags and home plate was a board.   Balltown played Buenie.   All I remember is the last inning.   Buenie was
ahead 7-4 and Balltown had the bases loaded.   Joe Brimeyer hit a
grand slam homerun to win the game.   The Buenie catcher was so
149

mad I remember him throwing his catcher's mitt into the back seat of his Model T Ford. Some of the players at that time were Joe Brimeyer, Joe Sahm, Arnold and Clarence Gansemer, Eldon Pfhol, Leander Klein, Joe Strumberger, and some of the Breitbachs. I also remember seeing Nanny Pape play at least one game. He was an All American football player at the University of Iowa and was killed in the line of duty as a State Highway Patrolman.

During that same time, I remember going to games at Granada Gardens in the Sageville area. They had a beautiful ball diamond with a covered grandstand. Around 1940 Cletus Link became the manager. Farley and Balltown never got along. They had many arguments. When Balltown played Cassville, Wisconsin both teams would party together after the game.

John Richard – Kieler

My baseball career lasted from 1955-77. I played high school ball for Loras Academy in Dubuque and also started with the Kieler town team at the same time. Originally we played in a league called the Pecatonica League which included teams like East Dubuque, Benton, Shullsburg, Platteville, Dickeyville, Lancaster, Potosi, and Darlington. It later became the Tri-County League which also included teams from Illinois. I also caught a few games in the Iowa tournaments when the local teams brought in a hired pitcher.

Some of the good players that I played with or against included Cub Speth, Jerry Jansen, Ken Townsend, Jerry Roth, Dan Sullivan, and Bill Burbach. I also caught Jim McAndrew in the Cascade Tournament in the early sixties when we beat Rickardsville, 1-0. He was pitching at the University of Iowa at the time. He could really throw hard, but he did not have much of a breaking ball then. I know he developed that later as he advanced into pro ball. The best pitcher I ever caught was Cub Speth when he played with us for three years. He threw hard, had a good breaking ball, and had good control. I remember one night we were going to a tournament game in Iowa when he told Jerry Jansen and me that he had a tryout with some major league team right out of high school. They offered him $100 a month to play in a Class D League, but he was told to hold out for more. He said, "Here I am 26 years old and I'm still holding out."

Hank Lucas – Holy Cross

For many years, I have had the privilege of putting on a baseball uniform. This started in Little League at the age of eight and continues to this day, over 50 years later. My years playing on a good Holy Cross team that had solid chemistry and tremendous fan support always bring back fond memories. I had the good fortune of playing semi-pro baseball well into my forties. Then I was selected to play as a Ghost Player in the *Field of Dreams* movie. After that I was a member of the Ghost Team that traveled to many different countries, representing the United States as good will ambassadors for baseball. For the last eleven years, I managed the Dubuque County American Legion team. I also help out with the little league teams in Holy Cross, as well as giving lessons to young pitchers around the area.

As a youngster, my hero was John Schiesel from Dubuque who pitched for the Holy Cross town team a number of years. I idolized him because he was a pitcher and a real quiet guy. I would always sit next to him on the bench and ask him questions. He would always answer me even though he wanted to be by himself and concentrate.

To this day, every time I put on my two baseball socks I say a little prayer for two of my best friends who never had the opportunity to ever put on a uniform because of muscular birth defects. One of them is in heaven now.

Baseball has been very good for me and I want to stay involved with it as long as I can.

Gary Langel – Worthington, Iowa

The Day Mitch Williams Came to Town

In 1999, Worthington celebrated the 50th anniversary of its semi-pro tournament. Many special promotions were added to the tournament that year, including guest national anthem singers, ex-players throwing out first pitches, and reunions of former Worthington queen candidates and tournament MVPs.

151

Another feature added just for that tournament was a 15 man closed roster for all 16 teams in the tourney. Managers were asked to turn in their complete roster prior to the tournament and use only those players throughout. As tourney director, I had the responsibility of obtaining the roster names from the various managers. When Mike Sherrman from Farley turned in his roster that included Mitch Williams, I never thought that it was the former major league pitcher. However, a few days later it was confirmed that indeed, it was the real Mitch.

Once that announcement was made, the drama really started to build. It was especially so because there was the possibility of rain-outs and Mitch was only going to be in the area for just one night. Therefore, many contingent plans had to be made, including make shift tarps and even possibly changing the tournament schedule to ensure that Farley would play on the only night that Mitch was in town.

The day of the game finally arrived and went off on schedule. The game itself was almost anti climatic. Farley's opponent, Rickardsville, batted first and scored three runs as the result of a combination of hit batsmen, walks, errors, and a few hits. Mitch struggled again in the second and third innings, and then left the game with Farley trailing 6-3. Upon being taken out, he went behind the Farley dugout and signed autographs, had pictures taken, and talked to the fans. He was the ultimate professional even after a not-so-impressive showing.

The large crowd, numbering over 2,500 stayed until the end of the game. Everyone went home happy. The fans got to see what they came for and the Rickardsville team could boast that they beat an ex-major league pitcher just two years removed from the big leagues. It was one of the most memorable nights of baseball at Worthington Memorial Park. I'm thankful to the Farley Hawks team for allowing it to happen and proud to say I got to be a very small part of it.

Jim Sauser – League City, Texas

I grew up in Worthington, Iowa and played for the town team a few years. I remember a game in the late forties when Cy Wolfe was pitching and his dad was umpiring. In those days, there was only one umpire and he stood behind the pitcher, so he could umpire

152

the bases and call balls and strikes as the same time. Anyway, Cy hits this long ball to the outfield and his dad is running right along with him, cheering him on as he's watching the ball in the outfield. He got caught up in the excitement of his son trying to get a home run. It was really funny. But the other team never complained about his temporary lapse from being impartial.

Diane Harris, Cy's daughter, provided pictures of her father's equipment when he was playing.

Extra Innings

Anecdotal Collection of Small Town Baseball in Eastern Iowa

This chapter consists mainly of newspaper articles concerning small town baseball. All articles are reprinted with the permission of the Newspapers they appeared in.

155

THE DUBUQUE COUNTY BASEBALL HALL OF FAME

Dubuque County Baseball Hall of Fame Charter Members

1987 — Hub Orr (Cascade), Joseph HOERNER (Dubuque), Chick Palmer (Dubuque), Red Faber (Cascade), Rev. John Moran (Cascade), Doc Hipschen (Dubuque)

1988 — John ARMSTRONG (Dubuque), Joe Schlueter (Dubuque), Lefty Koob (Dubuque), Luce Sprengelmeyer (Dubuque), Tom Breitbach (Dubuque), Robert J. "Bob" HOERNER (Dubuque), Noel Callahan (Epworth), Norb Dupont (Sherrill), John Brueckner (Dyersville), Lefty Meyer (Dyersville), John Sullivan (Cascade), Bud Kurt (Cascade).

1989 — Dr. Gene Hoffmann (Lamotte), Leo "Chief" Meyer (Dubuque), Rev. John Breitbach (Peosta), James George (Dubuque), Tom Jenk Sr. (Dyersville).

1990 — Walt Sprengelmeyer (Dubuque), Art Huinker (Dyersville), Gene POTTS (Dubuque), Doc Bisenius (Cascade), Ray Olberding (Dyersville), Dick Dupont (Sherrill).

1991 — Michael Sylvester MCCAULEY (Dubuque), Ted Bowman (Dubuque), Ed Schiltz (Dubuque), Bob Meyer (Balltown), Bob Krapfl (New Vienna), Ray Callahan (Epworth), Ernie Burger (Worthington).

1992 — Jim Hoerner (Key West), Earl "Ozzie" Brahm (Balltown), Del O'Hea (Dubuque), Jim "Popeye" Hosch (Cascade), Dale Digman (Worthington), Leo Schlueter Sr. (Dubuque), Leroy Gassman (Worthington). Honorary: Lloyd C. "Casey" HAYES (Key West), Bob "Ozzie" English (Dyersville).

1993 — Merle "Bud" Ross (Epworth), Rocky Schiltz (Dubuque), Pat Clarke (Cascade), John Deckert (Dubuque), Charles Plamondon (Dubuque), Ralph Buchman (Epworth), Carl Heitz (Key West), Rev. John Pitzen (Dyersville). Honorary: Gerald "Red" MCALEECE (Dubuque).

1994 — Dave Reittinger (Dyersville), Jim Roth (Dubuque), Merle Mathis (Dubuque), Justin "Judd" Driscoll (Bernard), Dick Schnier (Worthington), Jerry Roling (Holy Cross). Honorary: Vern Weber (Cascade).

1995 — Jim Digman (Dyersville), Bill Kelly (Dubuque), Rick Collins (Zwingle), Joe Pillard (Key West), Don Till (Farley), Mike Weeber (Dubuque). Honorary: Ralph Klein (Balltown).

1996 — Kevin RHOMBERG (Dubuque), Mick Meyer (Balltown), Ron Legrand (Holy Cross), Clarence "Doc" Soppe (Worthington), Milt Grawe (Dyersville), Dorrance Melloy (Bernard). Honorary: Louis Ruden (Holy Cross).

1997 — Jim Boffeli (Farley), Bob Schlueter (Dubuque), Jack Nicks (Dubuque), Fred McGovern (Peosta), Ron Hess (Dyersville), Joe Strumberger (Balltown), Gus Meloy (Bernard). Honorary: Rich Knepper (Cascade).

1998 — Jim Schmitt (Rickardsville), Joe Burger (Worthington), Pat English (Dyersville), Rev. Wayne Ressler (Cascade), Tom Byrne (Dubuque), Paul Kurt (Cascade). Honorary: Harry Leitner (Dubuque). Umpires: Jack Anglin (Dubuque).

1999 — Clyde Oberbroeckling (Holy Cross), Jude Milbert (Dyersville), Martin "Gue" Kennedy (Placid), Carl "Cuz" OTTAVI (Dubuque), Paul Schmitt (Rickardsville), Pete Welbes (Dubuque). Umpires: Fred Neiers (Cascade), Nick Pauly (Dubuque). Honorary: Merlin Simon (Cascade).

2000 — Joe Williams (Dubuque), Fred Galliart (Dubuque), Emmet Simon (Placid), John "Midge" Delaney (Dubuque), Dennis Roling (Holy Cross), Terry McDermott (Epworth), Leroy "Sal" Willenbring. Honorary: Paul "Winkie" Hoerner (Epworth), Leon Cummer (Balltown).

2001 — Joe "Heinie" Featherston (Cascade), Neil Bruck (Bernard), Jim Wegmann (Dyersville), Marty Lampe (Sherill) Terry Callahan (Epworth). Honorary: Loras Collins (Zwingle), Ade Kurt (Cascade).

2002 — Morrie Klocker (Cascade), Irwin Simon (Cascade), Ken Bruck (Bernard), Rollie Sampson (Dyersville), Jeff Potts (Dubuque). Honorary: Bill Sahm (Rickardsville), Bill Burger (Worthington).

2003 — Doc Locher (Farley), Ralph McDermott (Epworth), Jim Fitzgerald (Holy Cross), Terry Kelleher (Dubuque). Umpires: Emil "Mike" Stakis (Dubuque), George Stakis (Dubuque). Honorary: Ray Donovan (Bernard).

2004 — Buck Herzog (Balltown), Jim Doty (Dubuque), Jim Weydert (Peosta), Bob Green (Cascade), Bob Faber (Worthington). Honorary: Al Denlinger (Zwingle), B.J. Featherston (Epworth). Umpire: Ralph Teeling (Dubuque).

2005 — Galen "Jake" Emerson (Cascade), Jerry Lynch (Bernard), Loras Simon (Cascade), Roger Schueller (Peosta), Mike Gansmer (Balltown). Honorary: Don "Spike" Olberding (Dyersville), Bob Roling (Holy Cross). Umpire: Paul Vaassen (Dubuque).

2006 — Harry Banworth (Sherrill), Jim Kerper (New Vienna), Lenny Tekippe (Rickardsville), Ken McDermott (Placid), Kyle Maiers (Dyersville). Honorary: Gerald Feeney (Bernard), Mike Gehl (Cascade). Umpire: Harold Davis (Epworth/Cascade).

2007 — Leon Sigwarth (Balltown), Bill Pins (Holy Cross), Glen Naber (Dyersville), John Lehmann (Rickardsville), Tim Muntz (Key West). Honorary: Dick Vaske (Dyersville), Ed Burds (Peosta). Umpire: Blair Gleason (Cascade).

2008 — Mike Ehlers (Dubuque), Steve Olberding (Worthington), Lee Simon (Cascade), Bill Spiegel (Peosta), Ken Ruden (Holy Cross). Honorary: Dan Urbain (Placid), Bob Stumpf (Dubuque). Umpire: Phil Sheehy (Farley).

2009 — Ron "Hank" Lucas (Holy Cross), Don Meloy (Bernard), Kevin Hedrick (Dubuque), Kurt Wedewer (New Vienna). Honorary: Gary Dolphin (Dubuque), Vern Haberkorn (Dubuque).

2010 — Paul Scherrman (Farley), Dave Simon (Cascade), Ken Wedewer (New Vienna); Honorary: Tim English (Dyersville), Mike Clewell (Zwingle); Umpire: Dale Wiederholt (Dubuque).

2011 — Fred Martin (Dyersville), Bruce Maahs (Epworth), Dale Wilgenbusch (Rickardsville); Honorary: Vic and Mary Jo Budan (Dyersville), Earl Rettenmaier (Balltown); Umpire: Al Stoltz (Dubuque).

2012 — Dan Kennedy (Dubuque), Kevin Felton (Cascade), Chris Hoefer (Epworth); Honorary: Gary Langel (Worthington).

The Greatest Semi-pro Doubleheader Ever Played in Dubuque County

August 1997

By: *Gerard "Bud" Noonan*

In the book, *Shoeless Joe*, author W. P. Kinsella relates, "I don't have to tell you that the one constant through all the years has been baseball. American has been erased like a blackboard, only to be rebuilt and then erased again. But baseball has marked time while America has rolled by like a procession of steamrollers. It is the same game that Moonlight Graham played in 1905. It is a living part of history, like calico dresses, stone crockery, and threshing crews eating at outdoor tables. It continually reminds us of what once was, like an Indian-head penny in a handful of new coins."

On September 8, 1947, while a student at Loras College, living at St. Anthony's Home, Jim Brennan, Al McEnany and I went to the Julien Dubuque Baseball Tourney at the Fourth Street baseball park (Petrakis Park). Cascade was playing the Dubuque Elks followed by a game between the Dubuque White Sox and Castalia. We took the Fourth Street Elevator to witness what I believe was the greatest semipro doubleheader ever to be played in Dubuque County.

On September 8, 1947 Jim Brennan, Al McEnany and I went to the Julien Dubuque Baseball Tourney to witness what I believe was the greatest semipro doubleheader ever to be played in Dubuque County.

The *Cascade Pioneer,* in its edition of September 11, 1947, described the frames as follows: "Thirty-one innings of baseball were played that night. Hot torrid frames; pitchers shining like gleams in the orbs of youngsters at Christmas. Four great moundsmen carved niches in the fans' hall of fame – great in deeds of yeomanry; skillful when the supposed chips were down." The first game featured the Cascade Reds and the Dubuque Elks. Cascade had an excellent team during the 1940s, and I have always felt it was the best small town local

161

OLD RIVALS MEET AGAIN — After 50 years Earl Koenig (left) of Castalia, Iowa and Tom Breitbach of Dubuque meet after facing each other in an 18-inning tournament ballgame. (Photo courtesy of Charles McCormick)

1947 CASTALIA CUBS — Pictured are (back row), Rodney Anderson, Les Anderson, Virgil Monroe and Leon Everman; (front row), Tom Breitbach and Earl Koenig. All but Tom Breitbach were members of the 1947 Castalia Cubs baseball team. (Photo courtesy of Charles McCormick)

talent semipro team ever assembled. Three members, M. Kurt, M. Moran and J. Sullivan, played for the University of Iowa, and I am sure that J. Moran, the catcher, could have also played for the University, but he was studying for the priesthood at Loras College. The box score indicates that G. Hines (Monticello) caught for Cascade, so I assume that J. Moran was in the seminary on September 8. The Elks roster included Doc Hipschen, who played many years in Dubuqueland semipro circles and a strong right-handed pitcher by the name of Bob Chamberlain who was to claim the victory, 3-2, in what was classified as an upset. I'm sure that the organizers of this tourney were looking forward to a semifinal game between the Dubuque White Sox and Cascade, but this was not to occur. The Elks outhit Cascade 10 to 6, with Hipschen and Chamberlain each having three hits. Bob Moran pitched into the 13th and the *Pioneer* described his exit with classic 1940's journalism: "Moran signified he was tired, asked for relief. As Jack Donnelly came in from the outfield, taking the ball, Bob proceeded to the Cascade bench. It was then an ovation in intensity not unlike that when Jerome 'Dizzy' Dean left the mound amid the greatest din

of all time (it says here) when his 'nothin' ball threatened to stop those Yanks in the World Series at Chicago. Anyway, Monday, it was a *mighty fine gesture to Bob from the* thousands in the stands."

This game featured many outstanding plays by both teams, but the outcome was determined when Chamberlain was hit in the leg to force in the winning run. After pitching 13 great innings and holding Cascade to six hits, I'm sure he was happy to take one for the team. Following the conclusion of this game, the thousands in attendance felt they had witnessed a great game, but little did we know what was to follow in game two.

Game two featured the Dubuque White Sox and the Castalia Cubs. Castalia was a member of the Scenic League in Northeast Iowa and gained admission to the Julien Dubuque Tourney through the efforts of Verne Koenig, brother of Earl Koenig, the pitcher for Castalia. Verne was working for KDTH in Dubuque and knew Gerald "Red" McAleece, the long-time voice of sports on that station, and who was very instrumental in organizing the Julien Dubuque Tourney. The Dubuque White Sox were managed by Leo Schlueter Sr. and it was under his

Doubleheader cont'd on pg.20

163

direction that this team was to win five tourney titles. A great baseball man, Leo spent many hours on the Holy Trinity field in the early 1940s instructing this team in the art of baseball. A review of the White Sox roster reveals names well known in semipro circles in Dubuque, such as M. Mathis, B. Hoerner, and T. Byrne, but this game belonged to the two pitchers, Tom Breitbach for the White Sox and Earl Koenig for Castalia. In a remarkable feat, each pitcher worked the complete 18 innings.

On June 11, 1997, I made a trip to Castalia, along with Tom Brietbach and Charles McCormick to visit with members of the Castalia team of 1947. Mike Finnegan of Clermont organized the Castalia players and we met, of course, at the Castalia ball diamond. It was the first meeting between the two pitchers in 50 years. I asked them if they thought about "middle relief" in the 12th inning. They looked at me in disbelief and Koenig replied that around that time they were into 'the next day and had received their second wind.

Some of the statistics from this game, as obtained from the *Telegraph Hearld* of September 9, include the following:

1. Brietbach fanned 33 batters in the ball game
2. Earl Koenig, pitcher, had 18 assists
3. Breitbach hurled nine hitless innings, from the sixth to the 16th
4. Anderson, the 17 year-old Castalia first baseman, had 33 putouts.

Castalia scored the first run of the game in the bottom of the sixth inning on hits by M. Koening, Reisner and R. Anderson. The score remained 1 - 0 until the ninth inning when E. Koening retired the first two batters, gave up a hit to Bud Ross who stole second, and with two strikes, J. Kiefer lined a single into centerfield to tie the score. The large crowd in attendance settled back into their seats not knowing that the game would go another nine innings before it was decided when Ed Schiltz opened the 18th inning with a single, moved to a second on a bunt by Ross, advanced to third on a wild pitch and scored the winning run on a sacrifice fly by Kiefer.

Additional information discovered during this trip included the following: namely that Earl Koenig was contacted by Bill Prince, Chicago Cubs scout, following the game completion at 1:35 a.m., also that KDEC in Decorah, a companion station of KDTH in Dubuque, went off the air at sunset so that Castalia fans had to wait for the team to return from Dubuque around 4:30 a.m. on the ninth to hear the final result. I'm sure that Red McAleece carried the game in Dubuque until the final out.

It was also pointed out that on the 87th birthday of Leo Schlueter, members of the White Sox team made a trip to Stonehill Care Center to stage a surprise pepper game in the parking lot. This only convinced me that members of that team were not only very good baseball players, but, more important, "great people."

Since the games did not end until 1:35 a.m., Al, Jim and I did not return to St. Anthony's Home until well after 2:00 a.m. We had to ring the front bell and have the night nurse let us enter the building. You have to understand that we were young students at the time and later on developed other methods of gaining late night admission. The following day I was requested to come to the main office to explain our late arrival. I had anticipated the problem and took along a copy of the evening *Telegraph Herald* to help make my case. Following my explanation along with a copy of the story in the newspaper, I can still remember this good Mercy nun saying, "Gerard, what time do you think the boys from Castalia arrived home?"

❖ ❖ ❖ ❖ ❖ ❖ ❖ ❖ ❖ ❖

Reprinted with permission from The Golden View, Dubuque, IA

Before "Field of Dreams" Alumni Day—May 3, 1916

by
Tom Auge, professor emeritus

This was a special occasion, "a gala day," as a reporter from the *Dubuque Telegraph-Herald* noted. Shoeless Joe Jackson was in town, not as an image on a movie screen, but in person, to play baseball in Dubuque. For many, it was a dream come true.

On the evening of May 2, 1916, Jackson and his White Sox teammates arrived at a Dubuque railroad station. They had come to play an exhibition baseball game against the Loras College (then known as Dubuque College) team.

That the Chicago White Sox, one of the most feared teams in baseball, with three future members of baseball's Hall of Fame, would travel to Dubuque to play a college team may appear surprising. But Charles Comiskey, the tight-fisted owner of the White Sox team, was not one to overlook a chance to make money, even the relatively small amount resulting from an exhibition game.

Furthermore, the White Sox had close connections with the city of Dubuque and with Loras College. Comiskey himself had begun his professional career in this city. Clarence "Pants" Rowland, the manager, was a native of the Dubuque area. Finally, Urban "Red" Faber, their star pitcher, had been born and raised in Cascade, some twenty-five miles from Dubuque. Faber also had attended Loras College. The close feelings that existed on both sides manifested themselves when Comiskey invited the college band to perform at the opening-day ceremonies in Chicago the previous April.

The festivities on this gala May 3, 1916 began with religious services at the College. A parade from the school to the municipal ball field on Fourth Street followed. Two men on horseback carrying banners led the way with a squad of police next in line. The college band, which our exuberant reporters described as "one of the best in the country," came after the police. Carriages pulled by snow-white horses with civic dignitaries, White Sox officials, and the college faculty riding in them continued the parade. The student body, to the number of five hundred according to our hyperbolic eye-witness, properly came after the faculty with the alumni following. Finally, "a score of automobiles" brought up the rear.

The crowd at the ball field, in the estimation of our reporter, amounted to more than five thousand people. Furthermore, he was of the opinion that the entire town of Cascade had come to honor Red Faber. Factories and businesses in Dubuque had closed for the occassion. It was as if Dubuque had taken a holiday.

The band and a college quartet, using megaphones, entertained the crowd until the umpire, standing at home plate, introduced the pitchers. The hurler for Loras was Red Faber, loaned to the college in the hope of making the game more

White Sox opponents — Loras baseball team, 1916.

competitive. When the umpire introduced Faber, a delega-
tion from Cascade came on the field to present their hero with
a $100 gold watch.

The outcome of the game was not only what was anticipated, but what was also fitting—an easy 8 to 0 victory for
the Sox. The big leaguers had twelve hits, three of them by
Shoeless Joe, including a double. The best that our always-
positive reporter could write about the college team was that
they played well in the field, an observation which the four
errors charged to it belied.

If many in the crowd had wished for a better showing by
Loras, still the one-sided victory was what most of the crowd
expected, and even counted on. After all, they had come to
see the White Sox demonstrate their prowess and their heroes
had not failed them.

Alumni day ended with a banquet at the College, after
which the White Sox boarded a train for Chicago. As they
rushed through the darkness to their destination, they were
also moving a step closer to what fate had in store for them.
Urban "Red" Faber was to become a member of the baseball
Hall of Fame. Charles Comiskey was to be forever the owner
of the "Black Sox," a team which had sold itself to gamblers.
Shoeless Joe Jackson, an almost illiterate country boy, carried with him the ignominious role of one who had cheated
his team and his fans. But in the case of Shoeless Joe, in books
and film a more sympathetic image emerges, one which would
have been shared by the crowd that watched him perform on
that gala day in 1916.

Semipro Baseball Era Ends As Vets Retire

The end of an era has come to Dubuque with the announcement that Tom Breitbach and Bob Hoerner have stowed away their baseball spikes for good.

The two veteran ballplayers are the last of a group that brought fame to Dubuque as a city of fine semipro baseball clubs prior to the coming of professional ball in 1954.

Names like Schlueter, Eberhardt, Deckert, Braun, Mathis, Delaney, Bowen, Hipschen and Ottavi, to mention a few, dotted the rosters of teams like the Brewers and White Sox for many years.

The list began to dwindle after the last two clubs, the Brewers and Oldtimers, folded after the Dubuque Packers' Class D team came into being.

Some went on to play with other clubs in the area. Some were hired to compete in semipro tournaments at Monticello, Cascade, Dyersville and Winthrop.

But by 1960, only Breitbach and Hoerner remained active.

"I guess I knew I had it after the consolation game in the Dyersville tournament," Breitbach said. "I was called in to pitch for Balltown against Dyersville with the bases loaded and one out. I threw one pitch and Jack Dittmer hit it out of the park."

The fact that Dittmer was a former major leaguer and that he fanned the next two batters didn't change Breitbach's plans to call it quits.

"I think , I'm all done," Hoerner said. "I still like to play but when you get older and don't get any practice, your timing is off. It's no use playing if you can't do a good job."

Both Breitbach and Hoerner took brief flings in pro ball before embarking on long careers in the semipro ranks. Breitbach hurled one year for Janesville, Ohio of the Ohio-State League, and Hoerner roamed the outfield for Sioux Falls in the Northern League and Hutchinson in the Western Association.

The two veterans, who have competed with such teams as Cascade, Worthington, Key West, Dyersville and many other area clubs, have played a total of 38 years of baseball between them, with Hoerner claiming 20 years and Breitbach 18.

Although semipro baseball has long since ceased to be a part of Dubuque's sports activities, the names and deeds of many of the players have remained alive.

And even with the retirement of the last two "old warhorses," it isn't likely baseball fans will forget the thrills and excitement the semipro clubs offered in years past.

In Memoriam - Two Icons

Tom Breitbach and Bob Hoerner

Memories Passed On
(As told to my grandson Maury)
by Jerry Eberhardt

The Best Of Jerry

"A Half Billion Chinese Don't Even Know We Played the Game!"

With this memory, especially, Maury, Grandpa figures it will mean more to you when you grow older and read this for yourself some time in the future. This is because at that time you will better understand and appreciate what Grandpa learned from this baseball experience. (In the meantime, right about now, Maury, call "time out" and ask your mom or dad what the word "perspective" means because that's what this is all about).

Jerry Eberhardt with grandson, Maury Cohn

It happened one night after we lost a very close game to the Cascade Reds. They had a great ball club and over the years had become one of our greatest rivals. We weren't, however, used to losing many games. It had been one of those games when your opponent didn't beat you as much as you beat yourself. (That's what made us a good ball club, Maury. We seldom did that but it was one of those nights!) I had made an error at 3rd allowing an unearned run to score, and my team mates were guilty of a few other key miscues, costing us the ball game.

In the locker room right after the game I remember kicking a chair over, slamming the locker door, and throwing my glove! Grandpa lost his temper, Maury, but after all these years still remembers (and I don't know why) what a team mate said to me about that time. Our 2nd baseman, Bob Schlueter, (remember, Maury, I called him "Boom-Boom" in Memory # 1) said: "A half billion Chinese don't even know we played the game!" It's funny how a flippant, sarcastically humorous, off the cuff statement (yet so true) like that, at the time, can jar you into reality. It can suddenly put things into proper perspective. Also, another lesson to be learned here is that until you learn how to handle a loss, you won't really know how to act when you win!

Incidentally, Maury, we lost that game a half century ago and the population of China today has increased to a billion two hundred million! Hope you enjoyed this.

Love, Grandpa

Those who helped make baseball strong:

The story of Vic and Mary Jo Budan

By Brian Strom, Dyersville Commercial Sports Writer

In terms of pure devotion to the local baseball scene, perhaps none have had a bigger influence than Vic and Mary Jo Budan, of Dyersville.

In the span of 36 years, the couple has paved the way for local teams from the tot leagues to adult fast-pitch softball.

The Budans began their crusade of promoting "America's Past-time" by forming the tot league in 1980. The league consisted of 4-to-6-year-old players, who became acquainted with the sport using a rubber ball and hitting off a tee.

"We'd take anybody who didn't trip on their diaper," joked Mary Jo.

The couple was also responsible for reorganizing Dyersville Little League, and bringing it to its current status in the community.

The Budans also played a vital role in the building of Candy Cane Park.

In 1980, Mary Jo was hired by the city of Dyersville as recreation director. Her duties included scheduling games, managing the league and providing and fixing equipment.

While Mary Jo was busy doing the behind-the-scenes work, Vic took various coaching jobs that opened up around the league. Vic, a semi-professional baseball player back in the early 1950s, spent 36 years coaching area teams.

Among Vic's fondest memories from coaching was the 1985 Babe Ruth League team of 13 to 15 year olds that he guided through the state tournament and to the Midwest Regionals in Lincoln, Neb.

For Mary Jo, the friends and precious stories she has amassed over the years are what she cherishes most. While she received two awards recognizing her efforts in the community, what she revels most was a two-page, handwritten letter the couple received two years ago from a former ball player. The sender of the letter had lost his father as a youngster, and now was guiding his son through the introductory leagues of baseball. The letter ended with these words, "My only wish is to do the same for him as you did for me."

While the awards and love throughout the community were an added bonus, what the Budans were most interested in was involvement with a sport they loved.

"We're baseball people," expressed Mary Jo. "Maybe we just lived too close to the park," she joked.

"Yeah," responded Vic. "If there was a ballgame, we were there."

Vic and Mary Jo Budan have been an integral part of Dyersville Little League.

Independence Win:

DYERSVILLE, Ia. — Independence topped Guttenberg, 9-2, here Tuesday to win the championship of the annual Dyersville baseball tournament for the second year in a row.

In the consolation game Dyersville blanked Balltown, 7-0.

The final night, reigned over by newly-elected Queen Carolyn Rabe of Manchester, drew 6,389 fans, the largest turnout in the history of the tournament.

Independence took an early one-run lead as Jim Allen scored on an error after he had stolen third base. Gutten- **Miss Rabe** berg tried to come back in the third but failed to score after having the bases full and none out.

In the fifth inning Independence sacked the game away. Bill Rowland doubled and Orkie Sarchett's triple chased him in. Sarchett scored moments later on a fielder's choice by Bob Decker who tallied the third run of the frame when the ball was thrown into center field. That made it 4-0.

Guttenberg rallied briefly in the seventh on a bases-loaded single by Duane Hagen, hacking the margin to 4-2.

But Independence came back in the bottom of the inning with three runs on a double, two singles and a walk. The final two runs of the contest scored in the eighth on a single by Sarchett.

Jack Dittmer and Ed Watt,

both of Dyersville, shared spotlight in the consolati Dittmer belted a grand sl homer in the sixth inning wh Watt pitched a one-hitter a struck out two batters eve inning, a total of 14 in the gan

CHAMPIONSHIP GAME

Guttenberg				Independence
	ab	r	h	ab
Peter'n	2	0	0	Sarchett ss 5
Buelow 3b	5	1	4	E. Deck'r c 5
Hyde cf	4	1	1	Blum'ne rf 4
Rich'ds lf	4	0	2	John'n rf 4
Hagen 1b	5	0	1	Roth'k 1b-p 5
Hunkel 2b	5	0	1	Allen 2b 4
Neiers rf	2	0	0	J. Decker 3
Witford rf	2	0	0	Cieslelke lf 4
Turner ss	3	0	0	Rowl'd p-1b 4
Tangman p	2	0	1	
Totals	37	2	10	Totals 29 9

Guttenberg ..... 000 000 200—2 10
Independence ..., 010 030 32x—9 1:

CONSOLATION GAME

Balltown .... 000 000 0—0 1
Dyersville .... 011 011 x—7 7
Wolfe, T. Breitbach and Mey:
Watt and Kramer, Digmann G

★ ★ ★

Watt Named Most Valuable

DYERSVILLE, Ia.—Ed Wat of the Dyersville Whitehawk was named the most valuabl player as an All-Tournamen team was selected at th Dyersville Tournament Tues day.

Blair Beatty received the sportsmanship award.

Watt allowed just one hi and struck out 25 batters ir the 12 innings he pitched during the tournament. In addition he collected two home runs, two doubles, and a single in nine trips to the plate.

Those selected to the all-tournament team were: Gary Peterson, Guttenberg, catcher; Ed Watt, Dyersville, right-handed pitcher; Darrell Rothrock, Independence, left-handed pitcher; Bob Buelow, Guttenberg, third base; Orkie Sarchett, Independence, shortstop; Jack Dittmer, Dyersville, second base; Tom Jenk, Dyersville, first base; Gene Johnson, Independence, left field; Merrill Hyde, Guttenberg, center field and Ray Olberding, Dyersville, right field.

NICE SLIDE, BUT—Jack Dittmer of Dyersville, agonized expression and all, was out by a country mile (see umpire's "yer-out" motion) as he slid into the plate during Tuesday's consolation game in the Dyersville baseball tourney. Bob Meyer of Balltown dances away from the plate—but he'd already tagged Dittmer. (Telegraph-Herald Photos)

MY BASEBALL INTEREST INSPIRED
BY THE MAQUOKETA BEARS

Jack Marlow wrote the following article for the March 31, 2012 edition of the Maquoketa Sentinel Press. It is reprinted with permission of Jack and the Maquoketa Sentinel Press.

*T*elevision hadn't arrived. Our battery powered radio didn't pull in Major League broadcasts. I was ten years old in 1946.

Dad and Uncle Carl told me of the great Chicago Cubs, losers of the 1945 World Series.

The first real baseball game I saw was the 1946 Maquoketa Bears, a group of World War II vets, managed by Hank Streff.

The city diamond may not have been in playable condition. Early in the season the Bears played at Baldwin, Charlotte, Bellevue and Lost Nation.

The Bears lost their opening game to Baldwin, 8-3. The pitchers were Red Henson and Paul Morehead. Harold Hayes and Gene Bowman caught. Clarence Hike, Frances Dodd, Donald Schreiber, Don Hoffman and "Link" saw action in the outfield.

Write-up often mentioned "Link" without a full name. I think his last name was Lafayette.

Paul "Lefty" Byrne played first base, Ralph Nabb at third and shortstops Dwight Ales and Bud Myatt completed the infield.

Frank Reyner supplied the equipment. Local merchants and civic organizations paid for the uniforms.

The Bears defeated Bellevue12-7 in their first home game, attended by 800 fans. Nabb and Hike were the hitting stars with Morehead and Wilbur Neal pitching.

No admission was charged, but "silver" donations amounted to more than $100.

Bill Alden and Dick Streff joined the team during the initial season. One of the batboys was Haven Schmidt.

The schedule and competition expanded. The wins mounted. So did the attendance. One thousand fans watched a game between Maquoketa and Lost Nation.

The Bears held drawings for nylons and radios at games. Walt Dolch of Morning Glory Bakery gave angel food cakes to Bears hitting homeruns.

The Bears played two doubleheaders on Labor Day weekend, involving four teams. They beat the Rockford Grays, a Negro traveling team, 14-8.

A doubleheader was scheduled to benefit the construction of the Jackson County Hospital. Advance ticket sales mentioned an anticipated crowd between 3000 and 5000 fans.

The season extended into October when the Three-I League champion, Davenport Cubs came to Maquoketa and handed the Bears a 10-0 licking. Myatt and Nabb got the only hits.

The final record of the 1946 team was never printed, but the team had a winning record playing around 25 games.

It was just the beginning. The Bears installed lights at the city park in 1948. The schedule expanded to around 40 games against the finest teams in the area, plus Negro traveling teams.

The Prairie League All-Stars beat the Bears 13-12 in the first game under the lights before 1500 fans.

Games were publicized with a banner stretching across Main Street south of the Platt Street intersection saying "Baseball To-night."

With a batting order starting with Dick Streff, Lefty Byrne, Norm and Clarence Hike and followed by Bud Myatt, Ralph Nabb, Burt Distal, Dub Roomer, Gene Bowman and Larry Cook gave opposing pitchers little breathing room.

Heading the pitching staff were Jim Rankin, Wilmer Larry, Dillon Streets, Marcin Winchip and others.

Yet, the Bears lured other pitchers, like Whitey Rust from the Quad Cities and Mickey Fitzpatrick who was flown here from Rockford, Illinois.

Local product Gerald Koch once pitched nine innings for Preston on a Sunday afternoon and then came to give the Bears possible relief that night.

The Dubuque Merchants had the Bears down 8-0 in the fourth inning when Koch came in to stop the bleeding.

The Bears rallied to win 11-10 in 12 innings and Koch was still pitching.

Dr. O.L. Frank was one of the Bears' many managers. A player on a Negro traveling team hit a ball into the weeds in deep centerfield. He mocked the bears by circling the bases twice while they searched for the ball.

Doc responded by telling his outfielders to take a "spare ball" in the following innings. Later in the game the same player hit one into an identical spot, but nearly got thrown out at second base.

The 1949 Bears won the Monticello Fair Tournament, beating the host team and a paid pitcher, 17-6. Reports said much of the purse was left in Monticello as the Bears celebrated the win.

The 1953 Bears, aided by the return of Harold Satchel after his first season of pitching in the minor leagues won the Cascade Tournament. Ralph Nabb hit a two-run double for the only runs in the tenth inning against the Dubuque Merchants.

The 1955 Bears loaded up with talent outside their regular line-up to win both the Dubuque and Cascade Tournament.

The core of the original Bears were aging and new "blood" was needed to continue the strong reputation.

Pitchers Dick Adams from Savanna and Wes Johnson of Miles filled key spots. Graduates of the Junior Legion, Dick Clark, Lynn Socks, Larry Speech, Paul Ryan, Terri Herculean, Gary Battles and Bruce Comrade took up spots.

Yet, the Bears' 15 year run ended after the 1961 season.

The Indians arrive.

Maquoketa who once fielded three teams, the Bears, Cubs (Prairie league) and Clinton Engines, was void of town-team baseball for six years.

The Maquoketa Indians, managed by Al Denlinger, a Prairie League veteran at Zwingle, began play in 1968.

The team featured many high school coaches and experienced players.

Dick Wold was one of the premier hitters in eastern Iowa. Bill Fleming played shortstop. Bob Everding, Leo Hensley, Larry Bennett were joined by hard throwing Bob Denlinger and Jerry Jansen to form a deep pitching staff.

Ed Whitchelo, one of Maquoketa's finest all-around athletes roamed centerfield but could be used almost anywhere.

MHS graduates Cliff Cornelius, Jake Broman, Dennis Stringer and Tome Hence filled spots.

Haven Schmidt, after playing eight seasons in professional ball, still had baseball in his blood and played for local teams.

Denlinger, past his prime, was seldom in the lineup, but will be remembered for a pinch-hit grand slam walk-off home run to beat Sherrill, 7-5.

Dennis Burke, Dick Deem, Don Lyons, Brett Benton and Maury Wall were among those who helped the Indians along the way.

The Indians regularly competed for the Prairie League championship, once winning the crown three straight years.

The 1971 champions qualified for the ABC Tournament and were among the final three teams alive on the final day when they lost to the Waterloo Merchants, 16-11.

Denlinger retired as manager after 1973 and some veteran players scattered.

Brothers Dave, Tom, Bob and Scott Kirk, along with the Ichors, Adam, Eric and Ryan, and the Rosanne's trio Jeff, Jeremiah and Sage dominated the lineups in later years.

MCHS hit leader, Bob Gavin, Andy Wold and Mike Widely gave the Indians a lineup as potent as the Bears.

One season the Indians had five players batting over .400 and two others above .370.

Brad Manger and John Costello were pitchers capable of striking out a dozen or more batters in a game and Todd Conrad was a dependable hurler.

Finding a manager was always a problem. The team was kept alive at the twelfth hour many seasons.

Keith Croce arrived in 1993. Despite physical handicaps, Croce was living a dream and worked hard to raise funds and keep the team alive. He held the duties for 13 seasons before his death in 2005.

He had funds raised for the 2005 season and Bread Bickford took over as manager of the team in their final year.

I read stories of Maquoketa's early history when teams traveled by train to Maquoketa. The city hosted a weeklong tournament in the 1890's, drawing teams from as far as Chicago and South Dakota.

I wish I could have seen Frank Carson, Eddie Rick, Owen Frank, Flip Fleming, Emil "Dutch" Lesson and Merlin "Bib Foot" Lesson in a Maquoketa uniform.

I feel fortunate to have seen the Bears and Indians for much of the last 60 years. Watching baseball on TV can't replace those memories.

BERNARD INDIANS SCALP REDS

The following article was provided by Gerard "Bud" Noonan of Dubuque, Iowa and a native of Bernard, Iowa. It is reprinted with his permission.

The Cascade Pioneer Advertiser
Thursday, June 23, 1949

Fred Noonan brought his boys and a number of neighbors to town and whipped the Reds at the baseball picnic Thursday night. Five of the Noonans, a Meloy, and a Donovan combined with two who already strayed in from the north to gain a decisive win. Bill Noonan, F.J. Paul, "Bud" and Glenn all contributed significant action in the triumph.

Thursday nights' win also mended the break in a long line of Cascade victories over their fellow-county neighbors. Several of the Indians managed to swing their tomahawks a might stronger during the ball game, a win therefore could be understood.

A huge crowd jammed the expanse at legion Park to witness the conquest. The throngs saw the Reds leap off to a two-run lead in the firs inning. Bernard spent no time in erasing the domination. Scoring three times in the second, adding five during a fifth frame uprising, and adding one more the frame following. The Bernard nine enjoyed a picnic at the expense of several Red hurlers.

Meanwhile, Cascade had a Problem In. getting near many of Tommy Breitbach's pitches. Garnered by several Indians from his fold in Dubuque, Breitbach did a fine job of getting the Cascaders to give up hits. Tommy's support was excellent. The Reds' fielding was faultless. The big problem was in the hurling department where 5 of the 8 bases on balls resulted in markers.

It was truly a great evening for the Bernard Irish and their acquisition of Breitbach for one end of the battery corps, and strapping Dick Wertzberger, for the receiving end, didn't hurt any. Dick is a regular member of the Key West team.

Two of the Reds' runs were earned. Clarke walked to start the Cascade first. Dr. Eddie Bisenius powered a Breitbach special against the right field fence, Clarke scoring. On his way to third, Bisenius saw a relay pass overhead and into the crowd, so he jes' naturally came home too.

Second earned run was due to the big bat of Adrian "Trojan" Kurt. The little guy, who still plays as hard fifteen runs ahead or behind, tripled to right center during the fifth inning interlude of the locals. Again, Bisenius, an ace clutch hitter, sent the score up on a fly to right. Incidentally, the outer perimeter of the Reds' defense secured five of the six hits. Mr. Kurt got three for four, and Bisenius and Hosch each contributed one. Lasche, the third baseman, notched the sixth safe blow.

The Indians, when they didn't get free trips to first, proceeded to waylay Cascade pitching. The local outfielders spent many a busy moment scratching their bodies against the fence pickets. "Jake" Emerson tried his "banshee" stuff at the start, but the ball wasn't behaving at all, and those times it did, those rugged Bernardites proceeded to make living extremely uncomfortable for the Reds outfielders. Three other corpsmen followed the stocky right-hander to the hillock, and each enjoyed no privileges from the clubbing clan!

Paul Noonan inaugurated the second inning rally. His liner to left was for two bases. A walk to Ray Donovan, followed by Glen Noonan's two-base smash to left, opened the expanses of home late to the run-hungry invaders. Wertzberger grounded out, Hosch handling the throw. Breitbach was given a gratis excursion to first. The Noonan influence exploded in two instances to send the final of the 3 runs. Bill's was liner into left, and F.J. beat one out along the third base line.

Bleakness threatened to settle atop the Reds in the third, but nice pitching and dandy outfield support kept the braves from the promised territory. A walk to Paul Noonan followed a strikeout. Ade Kurt made a circus catch to Gen Noonan and Wertzberger preceded Breitbach's poke to center, which Neirs flagged down.

The fifth was a dream to the lustily-yelling visitors and a nightmare along the Maquoketa. Upshot of the five runs marked was Breitbach's long 3-base poke to dead left center. The bags, populated, emptied in a hurry after that blast.

Charlie Plamondon, one of the playing sages in the Prairie circuit, once told outside eyewitnesses that if Bernard had little help in their chucking, and probably reinforcements available in case of other needs, that team would be controlling part of the chase toward their loop flag. Mr. Plamondon has others who agree with him.

FANATIC FAN SOUNDS OFF
aka Baseball Mortal Sins

*A*lways swinging for the fences, especially with two strikes.

*C*onsistently swinging at the first pitch. Learn the strike zone.

*B*eing concerned about personal statistics. They can be too misleading.

*N*ot hustling. Giving maximum effort will neutralize physical mistakes.

*D*ressing sloppily. At least look like a ballplayer.

*B*laming the umpire--they are human too.

*C*riticizing teammates--no one is perfect.

*N*ot taking care of the body. Can significantly affect performance.

*N*ot respecting the dignity of the game.

*S*howboating. Act like you've done it before.

Their Proud Pastime
July 14, 2012

Eastern Iowa Hawkeye League All-Stars dedicate their convincing win to the Hall of Famers who came before them.

BY CLETE CAMPBELL
TH staff writer • ccampbell@wcinet.com

CASCADE, Iowa — The thriving eastern Iowa semi-pro baseball circuit was built on the passion of players who passed the national pastime down from generation to generation.

Each generation considers protecting and growing the game as their responsibility.

Many of the all-stars of Saturday night's 26th annual Telegraph Herald Semi-Pro All-Star Game took Legion Field for the boys of summer who came before them.

"Those guys were my heroes growing up," Prairie League all-star Chet Knake said. "I grew up watching those guys and seeing how much they loved the game and how passionate they were about it.

Chet Knake

"These guys could have let the game die. But they were passionate about baseball and they passed it down to us. It gets passed down to kids, and they pass it on to their friends. Hopefully, we can pass it down to the next generation."

The Eastern Iowa Hawkeye League wasn't passing up a chance to further its all-star game advantage on the Prairie League. Reaching Prairie starter Eric DeSousa for three runs in the first and sealing the game with a seven-run seventh-inning barrage, the EIHL didn't let up en route to a 13-6 victory.

Dan Spain

Game Most Valuable Player Dan Spain served as a firestarter, reaching base four times as the EIHL extended its advantage over the Prairie in the 10-years of the league vs. league format to 6-4.

The Key West star had Dubuque County Baseball Hall of Famers in mind with his performance Saturday.

"This (game) is about the Hall of Famers, and playing hard in their honor every single out," Spain said. "We definitely did that."

Getting five strong innings of two-run ball from winning pitcher A.J. Reuter, the EIHL never trailed. Three -run bursts in the first and fourth and the game-breaking seven-run seventh produced one of the most prolific offensive outputs in the game's recent history.

Chris Kerper's two-run first-inning single and Kevin Carkeek's two-RBI single in the fourth put the EIHL in charge early. Up, 6-2, entering the top of the seventh, the EIHL was intent on cranking up the heat on the Prairie League even higher.

The EIHL batted around and sent 12 men to the plate. Alex Timmerman drove in two runs in the onslaught.

"This group of guys plays with intensity every time they play," said Spain, who is keeping his own game sharp this summer while working to build his Clarke University baseball program. "It wasn't the score we expected, but we come out expecting to win every time we play.

"Guys take it very seriously. It's an honor to be here, and we put it all together tonight."

Four Prairie League errors carried a high price. Down, 13-2, heading to the bottom of the seventh, the Prairie League couldn't set off enough fireworks to get back in the game. Knake homered and coach Ryan Hoerner doubled and tripled for the Prairie League cause.

The eastern Iowa semi-pro game has become known for its high brand of play while drawing players both near and far.

"This is the best brand of baseball," Knake said. "I've talked to guys from Colorado and other states and they say no league they've played in has the intense competitive nature of this Midwest league."

As Spain said, "not many areas are lucky to have leagues as good as we have. We're fortunate to be here."

Today's All-Stars are driven to be tomorrow's Dubuque County Hall of Famers.

"It would be an honor to be in their shoes," Spain said.

• The TH All-Star Game survived the brief, but much-needed afternoon rain showers that temporarily led officials to cancel the game. As Legion Field quickly dried out, officials quickly rebooked the game for its scheduled 6:30 p.m. first pitch.

The Babe Ruth All-Star Game was rained out and rescheduled to today at 12:30 p.m. at Legion Field.

MATT MASIN • *Telegraph Herald*
Monticello pitcher A.J. Reuter watches a pitch cross home plate during the Telegraph Herald Semi-Pro All-Star Game at American Legion Ball Park in Cascade, Iowa, on Saturday. Reuter threw two-run ball over five innings to pick up the victory as the Eastern Iowa Hawkeye League beat the Prairie League, 13-6.

POST GAME REPORT
Bob Meyer

As with every worthwhile effort, there are trials and tribulations, as well as rewards. In this case, the rewards far outnumber the trials. The biggest reward was talking to many people who were enthusiastic in reminiscing about their memories and experiences with baseball in small communities over many years. Many of the people mentioned in the book were former acquaintances in my playing years, 1952-68. But many were not. Their memories and stories occurred after my playing days in eastern Iowa. Nevertheless, to a person, their recollections helped me relive those great years of playing baseball, which at the time, was like a religion.

Also revealing was the modesty that the former players communicated as they told their stories. The common theme was their memory of the simplicity and innocence of playing at the non-commercialized level, their dedication and love of the game. Although they still recall their individual accomplishments, most of them took more pride in talking about other players rather than themselves, an admirable quality of teammates and true competitors.

Based on this experience of talking to well over 50 people with individual memories and stories, it is apparent that these are just a small sample of people who also have interesting stories to tell. Wouldn't it be great if many more people could share their own experiences at some point as well?

An obvious question is: What is the future of small town baseball? In eastern Iowa, most towns still have a team, and there are ten annual tournaments. That is what is keeping it alive as Sunday ball is not as popular anymore. Also, the number of fans who attend games has decreased from years past. For example, the Dyersville Tournament used to draw over 5,000 people for the two final nights - the Queen Pageant and Championship Game. Now that number is under 1,000. Will it continue to decline as is true for many other parts of the country?

Todd Hospondarsky, a teacher at Monticello High School, recently completed a thesis on this subject for his Master's Degree at the University of Northern Iowa. Todd concludes that baseball has survived in northeast Iowa for two reasons: most teams have remained fiscally sound due in large part to the tournament structure that involves ten town teams hosting sixteen team tournaments throughout the summer. Secondly, there continues to be a desire to play baseball.

Todd concludes, "For whatever the reason, baseball is a key part of the towns in northeast Iowa. Some might argue it originates from the *Field of Dreams* site. I would argue the passion for baseball in northeast Iowa goes much farther back in time. Whenever it started, there is no doubt that there has been a deep rooted   passion   for baseball here that refused to let semi-pro die as it has in other areas of the country. There is a tradition here that is sometimes contained within a family.

Sometimes traditions lay within a town's past. Baseball has an undeniable connection with history in the United States. I believe it has a connection with the future of northeast Iowa. Managers will continue to organize and prepare, players will continue to play, and baseball will continue to live here."

*   *   *

I have deliberately tried to keep myself out of the book as much as possible because this is about other people. But since much of the content focuses on memories and stories, I need to share a couple of my own since they strongly influenced my college and semi-pro career. Both occurred when playing at Brooks Air Force Base in San Antonio, Texas.

Our manager was a crusty old Master Sergeant, John Springer. John was a true baseball man. He taught me how to play the game and influenced my philosophy about always hustling. He said, "Son" (John called everybody 'Son') whenever you step on the ball field you run." I never forgot it and always tried to play the game with 100% plus effort. I expected no less of my teammates and still emphasize that attitude today whenever I have a chance to mentor youngsters.

Another important thing I learned in those early catching days was how to protect myself. As a raw 19 year old, I was pressed into service as a catcher because our other two catchers got injured. Before that I always played shortstop. We were playing in a tournament in Austin, Texas. In the first game, a foul tip hit me in a bad place. After about five minutes of excruciating pain I finally was able to continue. When asked if I was wearing a "cup" I asked naively, "What's that?" All I knew was that a catcher's equipment consisted of a mask, chest protector and shin guards. Since we had an early game the next day our pitcher and I went into town early in the morning and knocked on sporting goods stores until somebody let us in. After my purchase, I thought that I was all set for the morning game.

Early in the game there was a play at the plate. It looked like we would have the runner by a mile. I was holding the ball ready to apply a gentle tag to the guy, a huge first baseman who was well over six feet and 250 pounds. As he approached the plate, with a little smile on his face, he just slowed down and gave the impression of giving up. The next thing I knew, I was flat on my back half way to the backstop. The ball, mitt, and mask went in different directions. My teammates later told me that this big fella just lowered the boom as I was standing in front of home plate to apply this "gentle" tag. It was little consolation that the umpire called him out for unsportsmanlike conduct. At least I learned another valuable lesson in protecting myself. After that, whenever there were collisions at home plate, and there were many, I was prepared. It could be said that whoever coined the phrase "tools of ignorance" for a catcher might have had guys like me in mind.

In conclusion, I have to agree with my friend, Joe Sigwarth, who says, "As a former catcher, there is nothing more exhilarating than hearing the national anthem, the umpire yells, "Play Ball', the pitcher delivers and the ball pops the mitt for strike one. This is heavenly and it is small town baseball."

Finally, I have pledged that any profits from the book, beyond expenses, will be donated to charity. I have selected two: The Christian Foundation for Children and Aging headquartered in Kansas City, Kansas, and Camp Courageous located in Monticello, Iowa.

Information on these agencies can be found at:

Christian Foundation for Children and Aging: mail@cfcausa.org or www.hopeforafamily.org.

Camp courageous: info@campcourageous.org

"You know, we just don't recognize the most significant moments of our lives while they're happening. Back then, I thought, well, there'll be other days. I didn't realize that that was the only day."

Moonlight Graham, *Field of Dreams*

ACKNOWLEDGEMENTS

So many people have been part of making this book a reality that it's hard to know where to begin.

My sincere appreciation to all those who willingly contributed their stories and memories that fill these pages. They are the heart of this book.

To the talented Colleen McKeon, my sincere appreciation for the time and effort spent on the cover illustration and the "fanatic fan" cartoon drawing. Her ability to capture what I envisioned, with only a little description from me, was amazing!

I am also indebted to some very select individuals who became my advisory group and "go to guys". They were an invaluable source of information and helped me make the necessary contacts. My deepest gratitude to Jim Brimeyer, Tiny Potts, Jerry Roling, Joe Sigwarth, and my brother, Roger Meyer. They are my true partners in this endeavor.

Countless others provided guidance in my first attempt at book writing. These include Dave Stark, John Leheney, Connie Nolte and of course, Rich Wolfe.

Lastly, but most significantly, I thank my family from the bottom of my heart. My four children, their spouses, and my grandchildren have given me the ideas, encouragement, and good humor that I needed to persevere. Special appreciation goes to Ruth, my good wife and an eagle-eyed former teacher, who scrutinized my drafts and gave on going support.